KU-522-914

Contents

List of figures and tables

Figures

Table

Acknowledgements

We have had support, encouragement and critical feedback from numerous sources during the course of this project. We are especially grateful to the Community Development Foundation for funding some of the expenses incurred by our regular meetings and to the staff of St Bede's Pastoral Centre, York, for providing a conducive environment for our deliberations.

A number of people have given feedback on the ideas for the book in its early stages, including: Dave Evans, Paula Farrow, Alison Gilchrist, Andy Glen, Paul Hendrich, Margaret Ledwith, Colin Miller, Steve Skinner and Yvette Smalle. We would also like to express our thanks to a group of practitioners and Masters in Community and Youth Work students at Durham University who gave comments on the draft model.

Some chapters draw on individual and group interviews with community practitioners. While the practitioners and their organisations remain anonymous, we would like to express our gratitude to them for giving up their time to share accounts of their practice. Their contribution to the book is greatly appreciated – adding a variety of voices from the front line, which clearly demonstrate the commitment, passion and skills deployed by those people who work (paid or unpaid) in the field of community practice.

Finally, there are our families, friends and colleagues, who have yet again suffered our participation in a long process of writing, rewriting, sighing and occasionally smiling as we have sent our drafts repeatedly across the ether and carried them, scrawled upon and dog-eared, to and from our rendezvous in York.

ONE

Introduction

Paul Henderson

This book concentrates on a critical approach to community practice. We think that such a publication is both timely and important for several reasons. The continuing emphasis on community involvement in politics, policy and practice in Britain is increasing the number and range of practitioners involved in community practice: local activists, paid professionals, managers and policy makers. For many, community practice is only part of their role and there is a concern that some may not have had the opportunity of specific education or training in community-based work. At the same time, there is an increasing tendency for the work and activities of these practitioners to be linked to specific policies and programmes, which may have prescribed purposes, targets, standards and outcomes to achieve. This can lead to a focus on technical approaches (the use, for example, of a 'community engagement toolkit'), which can be presented as being separate from theory and as value free. Thus it is important that practitioners have access to resources that will enable and equip them to think critically, to use theory and to reflect on their practice in the context of the prevailing policy, social and economic climate.

These are some of the factors that have led us to write a third volume on the theme of community practice, this time with a dedicated focus on a *critical* approach, stressing practitioners' capacities for critical action based on critical theorising, reflection and a clear commitment to working for social justice through empowering and transformative practice. This introductory chapter begins by setting out the policy context that relates to critical community practice. It then goes back to the concept of community practice, summarising its definition and specifying the main 'players'. It refers to some of the reservations and critiques of current policies before introducing the model of critical community practice and indicating the content of the subsequent chapters.

The rise and rise of community involvement

The extent to which community involvement has become a significant feature of UK government policy since 1997 has been remarkable. Over the previous 20 years the argument that government should take the opinions and choices of communities more seriously depended mainly on the persuasiveness of community development professionals and a handful of commentators. Now, the list of programmes in which the policy of community involvement is very evident has become extensive: health, citizen participation, neighbourhood renewal; and the list could be extended to include: community cohesion, rural development, community planning, housing, social inclusion and sustainable development.

Community involvement was not a new development in policy making but under the Labour governments it has become considerably more prominent. In a review of community involvement and urban policy, Chanan traces the importance attached by government to community involvement through policy and guidance documents over a number of years, particularly in the fields of regeneration and governance. The government's commitment to encouraging active communities has become considerably more evident since the establishment of the Active Community Unit in 1998: 'Community involvement is clearly a major part of, if not synonymous with, active communities, and the profile of this issue increased exponentially in the succeeding five years' (Chanan, 2003, p 9). There has been no let-up in the commitment since then.

The case for a 'double devolution', devolving responsibilities not just to the town hall but beyond, to neighbourhoods and individual citizens, has also entered the policy vocabulary. While not being named as such, it formed the basis of the White Paper *Strong and Prosperous Communities* (Department for Communities and Local Government, 2006). This document promised to back up its commitment to neighbourhood involvement in governance with a stronger legal framework requiring local authorities and other best value authorities to secure the participation of local citizens and communities.

Changing landscape

At the same time as the community involvement imperative has continued, the landscape in which statutory, voluntary and community organisations are operating is undergoing radical changes. We are thinking, on the one hand, of the extension of the contracting out of services to the management and delivery of services by voluntary and community organisations and, on the other, of evidence of the extent to which community workers have been drawn into supporting the work of partnerships and thus allowing them fewer opportunities to work at the grass-roots level. The survey by Glen et al (2004) found that a surprisingly high percentage of respondents (35 per cent) spent less than 25 per cent of their time in direct contact with communities. On the basis of this and other findings, the survey report's authors pose the question as to whether some community workers are becoming trapped or caught up between the organisational demands of partnership working and the support needed by community groups.

Both the above trends point to the need to clarify the nature and scope of community practice. This is particularly evident when the attention given by government to the voluntary and community sector is taken into account. The Office of the Third Sector in the Cabinet Office is in a pivotal strategic position to influence both the sector itself and the policies of government departments.

Yet there is a serious vacuum in the formulation and delivery of programmes and services. Our contention is that a robust theory of critical community practice can help make sense of demands and pressures. It will go some way towards correcting the lack of recognition at the policy level of the work involved in achieving successful community initiatives:

> Because the work is often hidden from the public gaze, it can sometimes appear that community achievements have occurred spontaneously, when in fact they have been nurtured over a long period by skilled practitioners. This may mislead policy-makers into an over-optimistic impression of what communities can achieve without support. At the same time, because evidence of outcomes isn't often analysed, improvement of practice is held back. (Community Development Foundation, 2006, p 3 of summary)

The argument for a more rigorous approach is not a matter of special pleading, through the vehicle of critical community practice, for intellectual stimulus and clarity but rather for the interpretation of policies and programmes so that these can be implemented effectively and authentically. There is, according to the adage, nothing as practical as a good theory. There is, too, the need to strengthen the theoretical dimension of regeneration, health and other training courses at both qualifying and post-qualifying levels.

As they engage with the chapters, it will become clear to readers that the authors draw upon a considerable number of key sociopolitical concepts. These are defined as they are introduced. For readers who wish to engage with the model of critical community practice early on, see Chapter Four.

Community practice: what is it and who does it?

In our two earlier books (Banks et al, 2003; Butcher et al, 1993), we described 'community practice' as including all those processes that are about stimulating, engaging and achieving 'active community'. It refers to practice that embraces but is broader than community work or community development. Thus it includes work with a community focus undertaken by people other than community workers, and embraces the development and implementation of community policies. The latter aspect of community practice is crucial to its definition. It means that community practice is concerned with institutional change, albeit not in isolation from practice at community or organisational levels. It is useful to re-state Sarah Banks' summary:

> What we have called the 'active community' is at the heart of community practice, with the essential role of the community practitioner being to engage with individuals and groups that could contribute to developing communities. The key purposes of community practice link very closely to current government policies, with the aim of promoting active citizenship in the context of a desire to revive democratic participation in decision-making. (Banks, 2003, p 20)

It is particularly important to reiterate that community practice is not seen as the preserve of any one occupational or functional group in society. Community practice includes members of self-managed groups, community workers, other professionals with a community focus to their work, managers and policy makers (see below). All these people and groups could potentially engage in critical community practice, depending on their approach and the circumstances of the work.

- *Members and activists in self-managed community groups and organisations:* There is a large variety of different types of community groups and organisations working for social change in their neighbourhoods or communities of identity or interest. This might include local residents' groups, the friends of a local park, disability action groups, campaigning groups against domestic violence or global campaigns for women's education or debt relief (for a range of examples of local and global campaigning and self-help groups see Mayo, 2005: Williams et al, 2004). If these groups and their members embrace several of the values of critical community practice (for example, working together in solidarity, aiming to challenge existing power structures and to deepen and extend democratic practices), then we could describe the active participants as engaging in critical community practice. For example, a Palestinian solidarity group based in a UK city aims to raise awareness of the injustices faced by Palestinian people and initiates political campaigns, educational and fund-raising events. The UK members are expressing solidarity with oppressed Palestinian people and supporting them in their struggles to assert their human, civil and political rights.

- *Community workers:* There are many workers employed by organisations who have a brief to undertake community work of some kind. Thus the term 'community work' is used to refer, for example, to community educationalists and community organisers, as well as to workers employed to focus on issues identified by communities. It is a term that covers a range of different approaches, including community action, community development, organisational and service development. Workers may or may not be professionally qualified in community work or a related field; they may have a wide range of different job titles (from 'community engagement officer' to 'neighbourhood regeneration worker') and they may be employed to work generically in a neighbourhood, or in a specialist field such as tenant participation, environmental action or health promotion (see Glen et al, 2004). In large bureaucratic organisations, such as local authorities, the scope for critical community practice may be limited, but there are examples of workers operating at a local level within a critical framework. For example, community development officers in a large county council have been offering training to officers and councillors about the principles and practice of community development. They are very aware of the limits of what they can achieve and of the tensions and conflicts in their roles (see Banks and Orton, 2007). While not achieving radical change or an immediate shift in a large organisation, these community development officers are starting a process of consciousness-raising and reflection among people with political power to enable them to start thinking about how to listen to the voices of local people.

A more radical change will be for the politicians and officials to begin to recognise their own role in excluding and oppressing the people they represent and work with (Freire, 1972).

- *Other professionals with a community focus:* This category of practitioners includes a range of professionals whose main role would not be described as community work per se, but who use 'community work methods' in their practice – such as social workers, artists, police officers, architects or planners who may have a community brief (Banks, 2003). For many of these practitioners, the concept of 'critical community practice' might be foreign to them. For example, a police community liaison officer, who sees her primary role as developing community participation in matters of community safety and diversion of youth offenders, might not have a commitment to raising consciousness about the links between poverty, unemployment and crime. On the other hand, there are professionals who have a very strong commitment to social change in the community context. For example, a group of professional artists who work in an artists' cooperative in a former mining village deliberately take on community arts work, often with a radical edge (for example, working with local trade unions or campaigning groups to design and create banners that were used on a May Day march and rally with a focus on strengthening trade union rights). It is noticeable how project teams working on government-funded programmes often see the importance of opening up the community focus of their work.

- *Managers of organisations with a community practice remit:* Some managers have a very clear remit to promote and support community practice. Those who work on community development and regeneration programmes would fit this description and there are others in, for example, youth work, health promotion and housing, who come very close to it. All middle managers, however, who are employed by organisations that relate, in one way or the other, to communities are well positioned to inject the 'critical' element of community practice. This is because they have access both to organisational decision making and to training and other resources. All of these can stimulate the critical thinking of staff. The key question, of course, is whether or not managers have the vision, knowledge and skills to lend their weight to opening up this dimension – as well as the commitment to develop their own critical community practice role. The importance of the middle manager's role in both community development and community practice has often been under-estimated by practitioners. Our argument in this volume is that managers are central to critical community practice.

- *Politicians and policy makers:* This includes senior executives, managers and politicians in local and central government, public, voluntary and private sector agencies who may be involved in the development of community policies, partnership working, or encouraging cultural change to make organisations more community-oriented. The category would also need to include 'opinion shapers', individuals who have gained prominence in public affairs and who are influential. Anthony Giddens, exponent of the 'Third Way' of political activity (Giddens, 1998), Robert Putnam, a leading researcher on the phenomenon of social capital (Putnam, 2000), and Archon Fung, who has researched and advocated what he calls 'empowered participatory governance' (Fung, 2004), are examples of this group. Included also in the category would be policy-related organisations, for example, think tanks such as the Institute for Public Policy Research and Demos, and commissions such as the Power Inquiry (see Chapters Two and Seven). Community-oriented policies may cover a range of areas, from neighbourhood housing management to the promotion of farm shops. However, for any one of these to 'count' as critical community practice it would be expected that key stakeholders would be involved in making significant contributions to the formulation of policy, perhaps through citizens' juries and other forms of deliberative civic action (Rao, 2000, pp 137–22).

It can be seen from the above that the main rationale for this volume on community practice rests on the need to have a stronger theoretical basis in which values and principles are made more explicit and in which there is a consistent critical edge. In addition, significant policy changes, especially those relating to community involvement, point to the need for further examination of community practice.

Reservations and critiques

Commentators on the community involvement policy and the work of community practitioners have begun to be more critical. Macmillan and Townsend, for example, have coined the phrase 'community turn' to describe the policy, arguing that it is resulting in the voluntary and community sector appearing:

> to serve as a putative solution to a number of governing dilemmas. It offers governments the prospect of addressing,

and being seen to address, intractable problems through welfare services provided beyond the state, which are thought to involve lower costs while being effective and innovative. (Macmillan and Townsend, 2006, p 15)

Mayo and Robertson provide a historical and policy overview of community practice, pointing especially to the unintended consequences of community participation initiatives: 'The history of area-based programmes provides ample examples to illustrate the varying ways in which policies result in unintended consequences' (Mayo and Robertson, 2003, p 32).

Taylor gives an extensive treatment of community involvement and empowerment within the contemporary policy context, setting out a number of challenges facing policy makers, practitioners and communities themselves:

> The problems of the twenty-first century demand imaginative solutions and the release of new resources, which may well come from communities. The commitment to participation suggests that the 'tacit' knowledge, resources and skills that lie in the most marginalised communities are at least being acknowledged as part of the solution to some of these problems; but how robust is this commitment to 'community' and can 'communities' deliver? (Taylor, 2003, p 12)

The kinds of critiques referred to above point to the need for any optimism expressed concerning the empowerment of communities to be guarded. The language and intentions are to be welcomed. The problems occur at the point of delivery: consultation with some communities is undertaken too frequently ('consultation fatigue'); participation on partnerships boards is often unequal, with representatives of community groups and organisations experiencing too much jargon, too many papers and too short a time-scale between proposals being made and decisions being taken. Funding tends to be too short-term and insecure to allow communities to organise themselves and build their capacity to sustain change and development.

From both the relevant literature and the experiences of communities, therefore, it is wise to insert a note of caution into the scope and aspirations of critical community practice. Arguably, individuals and organisations with experience and knowledge of how community involvement and related policies actually work have a responsibility to communicate key messages to policy makers and politicians at local, regional and national levels. They also need to share their experiences and knowledge with managers and each other – across the four jurisdictions. In that way, it should be possible to improve the context in which critical community practice is undertaken.

Introducing the model of critical community practice

The term 'critical' is used a great deal in this book and most frequently, from the title page onwards, it appears in the phrase 'critical community practice'. The latter concept needs unpacking, but before doing so it may be helpful to note two other usages of the word 'critical' that appear in the book.

The first relates to *engaging one's critical faculties in order to mount a 'critique' of something*. Undertaking a critique entails looking at community practice, or some aspect of it, 'from the outside', and treating such practice as an object of critical inspection and evaluation. The previous section offered some examples, and further examples of aspects of community practice being subject to critical scrutiny will be found in Chapters Three, Five and Eight. However, the primary purpose of this book is *not* to mount a critique of community practice as an end in itself.

The second meaning of 'critical' refers to a particular way of *doing* community practice. Being critical in this sense is about practitioners bringing a particular mindset and cluster of attributes to their role and activities. These then shape the processes used in doing the work. They also affect the outcomes of the work. This meaning of critical practice is emphasised by Brechin (2000, pp 26–47) when she suggests that the term 'critical' refers to three types of practitioner attributes.

First, it entails an open-minded, reflective and thoughtful approach to working with people – one in which careful attention is given to the context in which actions take place and the ways in which different contexts are apt to give rise to different (and often conflicting) assumptions and perspectives. Critical practice involves acknowledging the likelihood of different perceptions, experiences and 'takes' on problems, and this in turn requires a readiness to embrace (at least initially) a 'not-knowing' approach, and an ability to tolerate uncertainty. Such a stance is especially necessary in times of change and modern conditions of hyper-complexity. Second, it entails operating from a firm foundation of values and assumptions. These include a fundamental commitment to social justice, which leads to forms of practice that are both empowering and anti-oppressive, and are respectful of others as equals. Finally, all these attributes and values are the subject of continuous review – the critical practitioner is both reflective and reflexive, engaging in continuous professional enquiry and development.

This second meaning of 'critical' has been reviewed in some detail because the idea of mindset and dispositions also constituted an element in the 'model of critical community practice' presented here.

The third and most significant sense in which 'critical' is used in this book is employed when we refer to *practitioners developing and deploying a particular kind of 'practice model', to guide and make sense of their work*. A 'model', here, refers to a simplified framework of key variables and propositions that help someone make sense of a particular situation, process or system. Community practitioners create and use models all the time – to get a 'handle' on the situations, processes and systems they have to deal with. Sometimes they borrow their models from other people (for example, Arnstein's 'ladder of citizen participation' (Arnstein, 1969) is frequently borrowed by community practitioners when they want to 'get a handle' on a new initiative in community participation). At other times they make up their own models for themselves, crafted out of reflections on and lessons from their own experience.

The practice model of *Critical community practice* has four components. The first component, 'critical consciousness', deals with what we have referred to above as 'mindset and dispositions'. 'Critical consciousness' embraces the assumptions, values and dispositions on which the other three components of the model rest, and these are spelt out in some detail in Chapter Four, on the assumption that the other three components are only as robust as the foundations on which they are constructed. The other components are called 'critical theorising', 'critical action', and 'critical reflection'. The model is presented in a diagrammatic form in Chapter Four (Figure 4.1, p 51) and the reader may find it helpful to preview the diagram at this point.

Three particular features of the model deserve mentioning. First of all it incorporates a *theoretical* dimension. This acknowledges that skilful and effective practice benefits from 'know-why' as well as 'know-how' knowledge. In this book a number of theoretical ideas and concepts are introduced and put to use – the concept of social capital, the distinction between state and civil society, the idea of the 'learning organisation', and so on. We make no apologies for this – such concepts and ideas offer ways of thinking about practice, of 'reframing' problems, and providing 'tools for thought'.

Second, the model embraces a strong normative dimension. Skilful practice carries with it a responsibility to base actions on carefully considered evaluative judgements – not only in a technical sense ('x' will be the most *effective* way to achieve our goal under present circumstances) – but also in a normative sense ('x' is what we *ought* to do in the present context). In the model, it is suggested that this normative dimension properly includes 'ideals' (for example, social justice), 'principles of action' (for example, community empowerment), and 'desirable outcomes' (for example, emancipation from disadvantage, exclusion and oppression). Such values, it is argued, offer the necessary ethical and sociopolitical 'compass' required to guide the work of all critical practitioners – from politicians to citizen activists and from community workers to managers of community programmes.

Third, the model can provide the practitioner with a more 'holistic' way of thinking about their practice in a critical way. The component parts of the model (consciousness, theorising, action and reflection) can be thought about separately, but their full implications and importance only become apparent when they are used in conjunction with each other.

The stimulus for constructing the model grew out of dissatisfaction and frustration with the limited impact that contemporary community practice was apparently making to the conditions under which people in the communities they worked in lived. This seemed to be true both in terms of the substantive outcomes of such work (levels of social disadvantage, exclusion and oppression) and in terms of process outcomes (experience of control over the conditions of their lives). The question arose: what would a model of community practice look like that was genuinely transformatory in its impacts and outcomes, that would help practitioners in empowering communities to realise significant social change, and which would be capable of supporting communities to work together in ways that would make a real difference to the circumstances and experiences of their members' lives?

These 'big' overarching questions gave rise to a number of subsidiary ones. A trawl of relevant literature helped us to think about how these might be grouped together in meaningful clusters (Barnett, 1997, was particularly important here), and this, in turn, resulted in a model consisting of the four components. Constructing a genuinely transformatory approach to community practice resulted in an attempt to come up with answers to the following questions.

With respect to *critical consciousness*:

• If community practitioners are to move beyond a conception of practice as primarily a 'method', based on a technicist and competence-based view of their enabling and empowering skills, then how should they conceptualise their value commitments and social goals in a manner compatible with an 'other-directed' or 'non-directive' stance? (Chapter Four)

• What assumptions about the nature of human beings, community and society should underpin the practitioners' theorising, shape their action strategies and inform their approach to critical reflection and reflexivity? (Chapter Four)

With respect to *critical theorising*:

• How far can recent work by social scientists on the dynamics and working of power in society assist community practitioners in constructing a more authentic approach to community empowerment? (Chapter Two)

• If communities are to become successful in exercising more power over the conditions of their lives, then what lessons can be learnt from sociologists and political scientists about the directions in which social institutions and political processes will need to be reformed in order to support such changes? (Chapters Two and Four)

• Can recent theorising about participatory and deliberative democracy be used to construct robust strategies for 'participatory community governance'? (Chapters Three and Four)

With respect to *critical action*:

• Who are the prime movers – the key actors – who have roles to play in promoting and implementing programmes and projects of 'participatory community governance'? (Chapter Four)

• What roles do such actors need to play in creating the enabling conditions for community empowerment to flourish, and for the establishment and management of organisations built on principles of participative and deliberative democracy? (Chapters Three and Four)

With respect to *reflective practice*:

• How can community practitioners be supported in moving beyond the 'comfort zone' of their usual roles, practices and theoretical understandings?

• In organisational terms how can leaders and managers of community agencies be helped to embrace much higher levels of community responsiveness to (and control by) communities and citizens served? Can the idea of the 'learning organisation' provide a basis for the organisational reflection and learning that follows from the introduction of community governance? (Chapter Four)

From theory to application

The 'critical' theme is dominant in the model and runs through all the chapters. The early chapters (Chapters Two to Four) are lodged within a discussion of theoretical issues, reflective in particular of the radical democracy model of critical community practice, while later chapters (Chapters Five to Eight) are concerned with application: how different ideas can be taken forward in various community, practice, organisational and policy contexts.

In Chapter Two, Hugh Butcher explores the foundations of critical community practice through an analysis of power and empowerment. He relates this to the continuing existence of disadvantage, exclusion and oppression of communities, documenting the extent to which these afflict and divide British society. He develops the argument that only by engaging with power can communities work effectively to confront the social, economic and environmental problems they experience. He then explores three conceptions of power: 'power over', 'power with' and 'power from within'. He argues that a 'power-with' approach is in some ways a more radical way of combating the constraints and oppressions of the powerful than 'power over', because it demonstrates an alternative paradigm – how things can be different. It is precisely this way of considering issues of power and how they can be addressed that points to the reason why there is a need to have critical community practice. The chapter concludes with the author suggesting the key characteristics of this approach to practice.

In order to illustrate the different processes and choices that are revealed by an analysis of power, Hugh Butcher uses Chapter Three to present case studies of communities which have mobilised to exercise 'power-with' and 'power-over' actions. The examples also illustrate how community members have obtained increased power through the development of 'power within'. The case studies look at neighbourhood governance of schools in Chicago, a comparison of youth councils in Espoo in Finland and Lambeth in London, cooperative community enterprises in Leicester and Minster (Kent) and local participatory budgeting in Port Alegre in Brazil, Salford and Harrow. The author draws some tentative conclusions from the case studies about participatory governance and active citizenship. He underlines the extent to which empowerment emerges as a key concept in the chapter, thereby providing a useful bridge to Chapter Four, which sets out the model of critical community practice.

In ensuing chapters we tackle the planning and action implications of the theoretical material, especially the critical community practice model, developed in Chapter Four. The focus of Chapter Five is on direct work in and with community groups and organisations. Sarah Banks discusses two case studies of community groups – a self-managed city-wide asylum seekers' network and a worker-supported neighbourhood residents' group. The issues raised connect powerfully with the growing policy emphasis on developing social capital and mobilising active communities. While the two case studies are very different they contain within them similar features, notably the importance of education, consciousness-raising and mentoring/role modelling by experienced practitioners.

In Chapter Six, Hugh Butcher concentrates on the implications of critical community practice for those who carry organisational responsibilities for leading and managing projects and programmes in this sphere. Building on an analysis of the weakness of existing approaches to practice management, he identifies what needs to change, suggesting an approach that draws on systems thinking, empowering leadership and organisational learning. He argues that forms of leadership and management that are grounded in such an approach will achieve the most productive alignment between the values, theoretical assumptions and practical supports so necessary to secure effective critical practice.

From the managerial and organisational context we turn in Chapter Seven to the arenas of politics and policy. Paul Henderson begins with a discussion of trends within the global context, paying particular attention to the concepts of civil society and social capital. He acknowledges political scientists' and policy makers' growing doubts as to the health of representative democracy. This is related to evidence from the UK of political disengagement both at grass-roots and policy levels – and how the government has responded. Five ways in which the model can be applied in the political and policy context are then outlined.

In Chapter Eight the focus of the book changes from having examined the processes and activities of groups, organisations and the political and policy context to looking at practitioners themselves. Sarah Banks is concerned especially to discuss their value commitments and motivations, their capacities for critical reflection or reflexivity and their practical wisdom. In this way the reader is brought back to the centre of the critical community practice model, namely, critical consciousness and value commitments. In her discussion, the author draws upon accounts given by practitioners and relates this to critical community practice. The chapter concludes with suggestions as to how practitioners committed to critical community practice can be supported through supervision, dialogue and reflective writing.

In the concluding chapter, Paul Henderson points to the relevance of the contemporary policy context to critical community practice. The practice has become more generic than in earlier years because of the 'mainstreaming' of 'community' and community involvement in policy and practice. However, the approach to critical community practice is questioning: is the concept, as defined and explained in this volume, valid and relevant? Is the model put forward useful and transferable? By critiquing the model the author acknowledges the need for it to be developed further in the light of experience and debate. It is this challenging note that characterises the writing throughout. Chapter Nine reaffirms the stance, implicitly handing the need for further thinking, reflection and action to others.

TWO

Power and empowerment: the foundations of critical community practice

Hugh Butcher

Introduction

Our model of critical community practice draws its theoretical inspiration from contemporary critical theory, and entails a commitment to *working for social justice through empowering disadvantaged, excluded and oppressed communities to take more control over the conditions of their lives.* Development of the model has been motivated by a conviction that only through a step-change in their civic and political engagement in the democratic process will members of poor communities bring about effective and sustainable changes in the circumstances of their lives.

In this and the next chapter, the underpinning arguments and evidence for our approach are developed in as transparent and cogent a way as possible, thereby providing the rationale for the model of critical community practice outlined in Chapter Four. This chapter begins with a review of the ways social scientists have sought to theorise the types and dimensions of power; and then moves on to discuss the community empowerment processes used in efforts to combat community disadvantage, exclusion and oppression. Chapter Three presents five short case studies of critical community practice in order to illustrate the real-world relevance of the conceptual approach to power and empowerment presented here.

First of all, however, it is necessary to be clear about the kind of communities and community issues that are the primary focus of critical community practice.

Communities of disadvantage, exclusion and oppression

Social divisions and structured inequalities

The *raison d'être* of all community practice is, of course, to work for community change by enabling and resourcing community members to address felt community needs. Critical community practice starts from an assumption that the roots of many, if not most (but certainly the most keenly felt and intransigent), community problems can be traced back to patterns of systemic material poverty and disadvantage, social exclusion and institutionalised oppression that, taken together, are manifestations of structural inequalities and social divisions within society as a whole.

Social research shows that Britain remains a society divided by:

- Significant and enduring levels of *poverty and social disadvantage*. In 2003–04, 12 million people were living in poverty. That is to say, one in five people were living in households in which the level of income was less than 60 per cent of the average. This is twice the level recorded at the end of the 1970s. Income poverty is related to a variety of factors: unemployment or working in low-paid occupations, being over pensionable age, being disabled or homeless, being a member of an ethnic minority.

    Besides experiencing income poverty, people in low income households are also likely to experience a range of other disadvantages: for example, low educational attainment (75 per cent of 16-year-olds in receipt of free school meals failed to get five GCSEs at grade C or above); poor health (death from heart disease and lung cancer are, for example, twice as likely among manual workers than non-manual workers, and adults in the poorest fifth of the income distribution are twice as likely to be at risk of developing a mental illness than those on average incomes); and to be victims of crime (unemployed people are three times more likely to be victims of violent crime than employed people) (Palmer et al, 2005).
- *Social exclusion*, which refers to the wider consequences of poverty and social disadvantage, and has been defined by Walker and Walker (1997, p 8) as 'the dynamic process of being shut out of ... the social, economic, political and cultural systems which determine the social integration of the person in society'. It is a broader concept than 'poverty and disadvantage' (although the two are often linked closely together in everyday social policy discourse, as 'poverty and social

exclusion'), but Walker and Walker usefully differentiate the terms by reserving the former term to refer to the 'lack of material resources, especially income, needed to participate in British society' (Walker and Walker, 1997, p 8). The Rowntree Poverty and Social Exclusion survey (Pantazis et al, 2006) provides a wide range of data relating to the many ways in which individuals and whole communities are excluded from full participation in the wider society, for example:

1. One in five people rarely have friends or family round for a meal, snack or a drink.
2. One in twenty have experienced disconnection (exclusion) from one or more basic services (gas, electricity, water, and so on).
3. More than one in twenty are socially isolated (having no friends they speak to at least weekly) (Pantazis et al, 2006, pp 126–60).

- *Discrimination and oppression*, which are also closely related to one another, as well as to poverty and social exclusion. Discrimination entails assigning a negative label to a person, group or community (strictly speaking discrimination is about identifying difference, and differences can be positive or negative – but it is negative discrimination that is our concern here (Thompson, 2003)). Negative discrimination is often experienced as 'oppression', defined by Thompson as:

> Inhuman or degrading treatment of individuals or groups; hardship and injustice brought about by the dominance of one group over another; the negative and demeaning exercise of power. Oppression often involves disregarding the rights of an individual or group and is thus a denial of citizenship. (Thompson, 2001, p 34)

For example, the false assumption that 'race' offers a scientifically grounded (or even 'common-sense') way of categorising people into separate biological groups has, of course, given rise to a very wide range of oppressive impacts, including racial violence and stereotyping, derogatory humour and stereotypical representations in the media, inequalities in access to housing, employment and welfare services, and unfair treatment within the criminal justice system (Thompson, 2003).

Negative discrimination based on social divisions like age, ability, gender and class has also given rise to well-researched and documented oppressions of their own. To give just a few examples:

- Elderly people often find their rights denied on the ground of 'protection from risks' that arise from their age-related 'vulnerability'(Thornton and Tozer, 1994).
- Disabled people experience exclusion and oppression in society on a systematic basis:'they have been denied inclusion into their society because of disabling barriers' (Oliver, 1996).
- Women experience oppression as a subordinate group within patriarchal societies in many ways, including low pay, worse working conditions, the 'glass ceiling' and so on. They experience appreciably higher levels of child abuse and levels of domestic violence, and they carry appreciably heavier and more demanding 'caring' roles than men (Elliot, 1996).
- It has long been demonstrated that class position affects educational achievement (Reid, 1998), health (Townsend and Davidson, 1988) and a host of other life chances.

Challenging disadvantage, exclusion and oppression through community action

Social research has also shown that the experience of disadvantage, exclusion and oppression, of the kinds described above, are best understood and explained as the consequences of significant social divisions structured into contemporary society (Payne, 2006). These social divisions can be thought of as 'first order' and 'second order'. First-order divisions comprise the axial or master social divisions characteristic of a society's social structure, for example class, gender, ethnicity and culture, each of which is constructed and maintained through the exercise of social, political and economic power. Second-order social divisions arise as a consequence of the particular focus, form and mix taken by first-order divisions, *within particular contexts.* For example, the profile of social disadvantage, exclusion and oppression in a so-called 'sink' housing estate (note the exclusionary connotation of 'sink estate') in a large metropolitan area will be experienced by its residents somewhat differently to those who live in an ex-mining village still suffering from the loss of its main source of employment and income following the closure of the pit 20 years previously. These are examples of geographically based experiences of disadvantage, exclusion and oppression, and such experience can become a stimulus and base for 'locality' community initiatives and community action.

Collective community action is not, however, limited to action based on locality. Other bases for community action emerge from distinctive patterns of disadvantage, exclusion and oppression experienced:

- at different points during the *life course* (for example, by the elderly, or by young people);
- in different *cultural* groups (for example, by particular faith groups);
- among those who share common *interests* (for example, the threat of a shared reduction in key services).

Critical community practice is, then, about empowerment; it entails working with members of communities (locality, interest, culture, and life-course) in a way that assists them to mobilise, and effectively exercise, a greater degree of power when challenging the construction and maintenance of the social differences that shape their experience of disadvantage, exclusion and oppression.

Power

If empowerment is at the heart of critical community practice, then 'power' and its utilisation are at the core of empowerment. It is only through engaging with structures and processes of social, political and economic power that communities can effectively work to confront the disadvantage, exclusion and oppression that they experience – whether this is in terms of poor health, lack of well-paid jobs, blighted environments, inadequate provision of public services, social isolation, personal insecurity and violence, and so forth.

So, what is power? Like most key concepts in the social sciences the concept of power is highly contested – that is to say its meaning will vary according to the 'paradigm' or theoretical 'frame of reference' in which it is embedded and used – whether this be, for example, the functionalist, conflict, or interactionist paradigms used by sociologists, or the range of meanings given to it within other academic disciplines (for example political science, psychology, economics), or social practices (community development, counselling, education, organisational development). At root, critical community practice is about communities using power to bring about significant change in the conditions of their members' lives through their own actions. We have found two rather different conceptions of power helpful in our thinking about community empowerment: 'power over' and 'power with'.

'*Power over*' entails an analysis of power in terms of the power of 'constraint' or 'domination'. 'Power over' is what many people think of first when they try to define power in organisations, or politics, or communities. It is action backed by authority, coercion, domination, or force (or the threat of their use) in order to overcome opposition and ensure that the goals of the powerful are achieved. It is this notion of overcoming resistance, in the context of conflicts over interests and/or values, that is the kernel of 'power over'. It exemplifies the 'win-lose' kind of thinking that underpins the so-called 'zero-sum' conception of power. So, for example, in community politics, those who can control resources, decision-making agendas, or how things are 'defined' can exercise 'power over' those who do not have control over such resources. Many see this as a somewhat restricted view of power, and community practitioners have looked for more positive, collaborative, ways of thinking about and working with power. This leads to the idea of 'power with'.

'*Power with*', on the other hand, is about finding common ground in situations where there is a conflict of interest and/or values. An outcome is sought that constitutes a 'win-win' resolution for the parties concerned. 'Win-win' is not, ideally, about 'compromise' (that is a zero-sum term). It should not involve any parties 'giving up' something; it does not rest, in other words, on a zero-sum conception of power – that there is only a fixed amount of it 'to go round' and that in order to resolve a difference and 'move on' one or both parties have to give up something. Seeing power in the alternative 'variable', non zero-sum, way allows a resolution of difference and problems that all parties find can meet their needs and concerns. This generally requires that, after concerted dialogue in which all parties become clearer and more 'appreciative' about how others 'see' things, an agreement is reached to 're-frame' the problem in a way that substantially reduces the conflict.

The next two subsections provide an overview of theories of power that reflect the 'power-over' and the 'power-with' perspectives.

Power as constraint and domination: 'power over'

Power over decision making, agenda setting and preference formation: A good starting point for understanding the idea of 'power over' is the classic definition of power offered by sociologist Max Weber, who wrote that power 'is the probability that a person will be able to carry out his or her own will in the pursuit of goals of action, regardless of resistance' (Weber, 1947, p 152).

This definition clearly points up the 'power-over' characteristic of this notion of power; this way of thinking about power is predicated on an assumption of a conflict of goals that ultimately derives from differences of interest and/or values and that constraining or coercive power has to be used by the parties to the conflict if they are to achieve a satisfactory outcome for themselves.

C. Wright Mills, in his classic *The sociological imagination*, put Weber's rather formalistic and bald definition of 'power over' into a more general social context:

> 'Power', as the term is now generally used in the social sciences, has to do with whatever decisions men [*sic*] make about the arrangements under which they live, and about the events which make up the history of their period ... in so far as such decisions are made (and in so far as they could be but are not) the problem of who is involved in making them (or not making them) is the basic problem of power. (Mills, 2000, p 50)

Mills here usefully distinguishes two 'dimensions' of power – he sees it as being about actual decision making, but also as about *non-decision making*, about how the powerful can use their power to ensure that potentially 'difficult' issues do not get onto decision-making agendas in the first place. (It is also worth noting that Mills was writing in the middle of the twentieth century – *The Sociological Imagination* was first published in 1956; from the perspective of the 21st century the reference to 'men' in the quote also underscores the importance of a further dimension of power. Power is inscribed in discourse; it becomes embedded in the very language that we use, and thereby subtly, but also very significantly, enhances the power of particular interests. We return to the power of discourse below.)

Stephen Lukes developed this 'multi-dimensional' idea of power in a systematic and rigorous way in his much quoted analysis of the 'radical view' of power (Lukes, 2003). He argues that there are three dimensions (or what might be called 'faces') of power:

1. Power as decision making: In this first 'dimension', power is effectively deployed by (two or more) participants to ensure that an overt conflict of interest between them is resolved in their favour. In this first 'face' the exercise of power is relatively observable and measurable. Such power is readily observed in formal organisations – the council committee, or the school governing body, for example. As Lukes says, 'the one-dimensional view of power involves a focus on *behaviour* in the making of *decisions* on issues over which there is

an observable *conflict* of (subjective) interests, seen as express policy preferences, revealed by political participation' (Lukes, 2003, p 19).

2. Lukes' second dimension of power concerns 'non-decision making'. It includes aspects of the first dimension but in this 'second face' power does not have to be observably deployed, though its exercise does ensure that decisions are made which reflect the interests of the powerful. Here power is used to prevent crucial issues getting to the decision-making stage in the first place.

3. Power as the ability to mould the desires, wishes and felt needs of the less powerful represents Lukes' third dimension of power. In this third face of power, preferences are shaped through the supremacy of particular values, norms, and 'common-sense' beliefs and ideologies. Significant issues not only fail to appear on the decision-makers agenda paper, but they routinely do not even arise in the minds and consciousness, at least in any coherent way, of many of those who have a direct interest in such issues; they are just not 'consciously thought about'. This form of power effectively shapes how people understand their world, and themselves, to the detriment of the interests of subordinate groups and to the benefit of the interests of the more powerful. In this connection, Lukes refers to the political writings of Gramsci, a leading Marxist of the early 20th century, who was influential in promoting a version of this view of power. Dissatisfied with some older theories – that 'the ruling class' relied on force and coercion as the main instruments of their 'rule' – as being far too simplistic (at least as far as modern industrialised societies were concerned), Gramsci focused attention on the importance of ideological and cultural control in determining and reinforcing beliefs and perceptions of what was 'natural' and 'given'. Such 'hegemonic' power entailed the permeation of a system of values and beliefs throughout society in a way that supported the status quo, and served to justify existing class and power relations.

The power of language: As already noted, a further important and influential perspective on power highlights the significance of language and discourses on power relations. Language works in an analogous way to Lukes' third dimension of power – serving to unconsciously limit and constrain how people interpret their experience of the world. Language provides a very powerful tool through which people can help make their world comprehensible and meaningful; it provides a means of ordering things and events. But it not only provides constructs and frameworks of meaning, and a syntax and vocabulary through which evaluations and judgements can be made about what is going on around them (as well as what is going on 'within' them), it also provides a means of communicating with others, and thereby of acting on and manipulating their world. The importance of this insight and its relevance to questions of power is neatly brought out by Dale Spender, in her book *Man made language*, as follows:

> Through my language and socialisation I did learn to see as *sensible* many arrangements in my society which an 'outsider' (who did not share my socialisation) would find absurd. So at one stage I did learn, for example, that it was sensible to give least educational experience to those who appeared to take longer to learn. I did learn that it was sensible to classify some skin pigmentation as possessing mystical powers. I did learn that it was sensible that one half of the population should be paid for their work while the other half should not. I did learn that it was sensible to ensure the survival of the species by amassing a vast arsenal that could destroy the planet many times over. And I did learn that it was sensible to see men as superior. (Spender, 1990, p 3)

This extract from Spender also illustrates how the idea of 'discourse' takes our understanding of the relationship between language and power a stage further. A discourse is a *particular*

> set of meanings, metaphors, representations, images, stories, statements and so on that in some way together produce a *particular* version of events. It refers to a *particular* picture that is painted of an event (or person or class of persons), a *particular* way of representing them in a *particular* light. (Burr, 2003, p 48, emphasis added)

As Foucault showed (2001[1970]) discourses affect our views on all things; it is not possible to escape discourse. A familiar example is how two distinct discourses can be deployed about a guerrilla movement, which can be described within one discourse as 'freedom fighters' and within another as 'terrorists'. Another example is illustrated by the current heated debate between those who espouse the discourse of 'intelligent design' and those who keep faith with modern evolutionary theory. Each discourse provides the vocabulary, expressions and also the 'style' needed to communicate and contest these world views (which then get played out, incidentally, within another set of discourses – those that lie behind and inform disputes about the 'proper' curriculum to be followed in state-funded schools).

Integrative power: 'power with'

The basis of 'power with' – what Boulding (1989) calls integrative power – is to be found in the bonds that hold people together in groups, communities, organisations and societies. Such bonds are vitally important. Psychologists like Abraham Maslow (Maslow, 1968) have shown that, after a human being's basic survival needs have been met, their next most pressing need is for 'belonging', for integration into one or more human groups.

> The most fundamental aspect of our biological origins is our social nature. Indeed there is no doubt that our ancestors were *social* before they were human, and consequently the greatest human need that we all have is for social bonding. (Clark, 1990, p 48)

Integrative power is, then, the capacity to achieve goals *with* others, not *at the expense of* others. It involves working together as a collective entity in a common cause, and the very *process* of working together, along with the bonds that both underpin it and are strengthened by it, are one of the positive benefits and rewards that accrue from working with this form of power. This is what makes 'power with' so effective as a means of achieving collective goals. Also note that this kind of power is dispersed, and with dispersal comes a cumulative widening and an increased involvement of people in exercising power. It is in this sense that integrative power is 'non-zero sum'. As the collective 'capacity to implement' (by individuals, groups, communities, organisations and polities) increases, so then does aggregative power.

'Power over' and 'power with' – similarities and differences

It would appear that these two conceptions of power are totally different; however, both conceptions share an important feature in common – they both resist conceptualising power as something that *inheres* in powerful 'individuals' or 'groups' or 'organisations' or other 'entities'. Power is understood as a characteristic of the *relationships between* entities in particular contexts. To say that the chief executive of a large multinational has immense power – as demonstrated when he or she makes a decision to relocate a production plant from the UK to a country with lower labour costs – is to use a form of shorthand. The CEO's power to implement the decision arises as a result of their position in a network of formal and informal relations within a specific enterprise, as well as within the network of economic relations that make up the particular market within which their enterprise operates.

We have already touched upon the most significant way in which the two models differ; it concerns whether power is seen as 'fixed' or 'variable' (zero-sum, or non zero-sum). To clarify further, if an individual, group or organisation sees the distribution of power in zero-sum terms then they work on the assumption that a gain in their power must mean an equal loss of power to the other individual, group or organisation with which they have a power relation. Power is seen as finite, as a 'constant'. It gives rise to the 'win-lose' attitude and approach to problem solving in conflict situations. If two neighbourhoods are competing to win a particular resource, then in a zero-sum power battle they will regard each other as opponents, as adversaries to be defeated: there will be a winner and a loser. A non zero-sum ('win-win', or cooperative) approach to power relations starts from the opposite assumption, that if both parties to a conflict look for, and find, ways to cooperate then a victory for both 'sides' can be realised.

'Power from within'

One further conception of power is worth noting. This is the idea of power as a sense of personal agency or efficacy (Dweck, 1999), about having the confidence and ability to act on the basis of a recognition that it *is* possible to mobilise (through one's own personal resource, or via collective action with others), and then exercise, power in an effective way. This kind of power is non-zero sum – confidence in one's potential to act 'powerfully' need not be gained or developed at the expense of anyone else.

Empowerment

Understanding empowerment: power-over and power-with strategies

When we define community practice as 'empowering people to take control over the condition of their own lives in community', then critical community practice is, first, about recognising how differential access to (social, political, and economic) power accounts for the disadvantage, exclusion and oppression of some groups over others. Second, it is about understanding how power can to be mobilised to achieve the resource redistribution and service improvements that will help reduce such poverty and exclusion, and confront racism, sexism and all the other 'isms' that underlie the experience of discrimination and oppression in society. Third, critical community practice is about developing the *capacities and motivation* that will, as a fourth point, enable the construction and *implementation of successful strategies* that will effectively challenge the power relations that undergird constraint and oppression.

Using the conceptions and dimensions of power introduced above, it can be see that in general terms strategies for empowerment will vary according to:

- whether the particular working context (the 'problem' or issue, the power dynamics at play in the situation and so on) offers a *choice* between strategies informed by 'power-over' and 'power-with' based empowerment; and
- if a choice *is* available, whether a reasoned *preference* for working with 'power-over' or 'power-with' strategies to confront the problem presents itself.

In 'power-over' approaches to empowerment the community practitioner's task is to work with the community in order to effectively mobilise it to *resist* the constraints and oppressions of the powerful. This generally involves working to develop and deploy 'influence' strategies (persuasive appeals to values, expertise, media campaigns, etc), the threat or use of economic sanctions (boycotts), invoking processes for administrative review or legal redress (use of 'ombudsmen', invoking processes of judicial review, etc), and so on. However, it must be remembered that communities of the disadvantaged, excluded and oppressed will, *by definition*, be in a position of relative weakness in any 'win-lose' power struggle. This is not to say that 'power-over' strategies are necessarily to be avoided – they may constitute the only available option, or they may be used as part of a 'mixed' or 'phased' strategy, alongside a number of 'power-with' approaches.

However, empowerment through deployment of 'power-with' approaches is in many respects a more 'radical' way of combating the constraints and oppressions of the powerful. By not even attempting to 'buy into' the dominant (win-lose, zero-sum) concept of power in our society, an alternative power paradigm is invoked, thereby opening up new ways of thinking and acting, as well as prefiguring, through successfully demonstrating its deployment, how things can be different. Because 'power-with' strategies are based on an 'expansion' of power, they are somewhat less likely to be perceived as a significant threat to the already powerful. Such strategies generally involve crafting new forms of social organisation within the state sector (for example, via co-governance, partnership working) and civil society (for example, autonomous user-controlled organisations), which both:

- enable the disadvantaged, exclude and oppressed to 'by-pass' some of the constraints and oppressions that they have hitherto experienced as part of the 'normal' social arrangements in their society, and
- demonstrate how new and alternative social arrangement might be fostered in a 'win-win' way.

Community empowerment: processes and tactics

The analysis of 'power' outlined here offers us a number of insights and concepts useful to understanding and implementing processes and tactics integral to either 'power-over' or 'power-with' strategies. These processes and tactics are outlined as a set of discrete 'steps' below, though this metaphor must be treated with caution. As will become clear in the series of case examples of 'power-with' strategies presented in Chapter Three, any real-world approach to developing and using a power-based strategy to advance social change will rarely unfold in the smooth step-by-step fashion implied here.

1. *Challenging ideological and discursive supports to the status quo*: Empowerment is about developing the confidence to question, and then challenge, the everyday 'stories' and 'taken-for-granted understandings' and discourses that circulate in society about disadvantage, exclusion and oppression. Do these stories and understandings accurately reflect community members' own experience, as well as those of their friends and families and fellow community members? Do they 'stand up' in the light of impartially collected data and evidence? Are they internally consistent and coherent? Do alternative stories and understandings and discourses seem to more meaningfully and more accurately reflect their experience, and better account for the evidence? What about the language used in telling the stories and constructing their understandings – does this work to unconsciously limit and constrain how community members interpret their experiences of the world? Will an alternative language open the door to alternative

interpretations that are at once less oppressive *and* potentially liberating?

2. Deploying critical consciousness in the way just described helps alternative 'constructions of reality' to be formulated, shared, debated and refined and to become established as new 'common sense'. The development of new ways of seeing the world and new interpretations of experience can be enormously empowering. It is likely that the interpretations of the powerful will be more or less self-serving and 'skewed'; there is every chance that they will involve stereotyping, 'put-downs' and negative interpretations. Realising that it is no longer necessary to carry the burden of such misinterpretations can be highly liberating – thereby enhancing self-respect, and generating the indignation and anger that will help fuel future action for change.

3. The above processes contribute, in turn, towards *developing 'power from within'* – that crucial sense of agency touched upon above, which can act as a vital motivational support for 'empowered' action.

4. None of the above is likely to be achieved wholly through individual self-reflection; it mostly comes about through *sharing and exploring experiences with others*, through conversations, and what Mercer (2000) calls 'interthinking' (thinking together); and it also develops through imagining alternative futures, teasing out how such futures might be realised, and taking tentative steps towards realising them.

   Involvement in small informal community groups can greatly facilitate these processes. This has long been recognised by community practitioners, who assist such *small group reflection and imagining* by helping to bring together groups to discuss issues that their members feel are important, in a manner that is open and supportive rather than structured and controlling.

5. Whereas small groups may tend to focus on the needs of their members, community organisations are concerned with building the foundations from which members can look outwards and develop a structure and strategy for effectively engaging with key players in their wider organisational environment. For community organisations intent on pursuing a campaign change-strategy, 'power-over' perspectives will require attention to be focused on ways of mobilising the most effective resource base on which to engage in a zero-sum struggle. For example, if sheer numbers of supporters are likely to provide the edge (for example, in running successful mass protests, consumer boycotts or rent strikes) then a solid membership base is a must; other tactics can include forming strategic alliances with other large-membership organisations.

On the other hand, if challenging the opposition by 'winning the argument' in the court of public opinion is deemed to be the most effective way forward, then investment in research and inquiry based activities, along with energetic and imaginative publicity campaigns and skilful public relations, is likely to be a priority for development and investment.

For community organisations intent on pursuing their goals within a 'power-with' frame of reference, a different set of problems and organisational priorities will present themselves. For example, planning and running independent not-for-profit demonstration projects designed to show the feasibility of new ways of meeting social housing needs or the needs of single teenage parents, or mounting an innovatory training and advocacy service for a socially isolated and excluded ethnic minority community, will require different kinds of project planning skills, specialist staff, and material resources. These too will also necessitate 'looking outside' to form networks and alliances with other service delivery, quality assurance and funding agencies. Achieving co-governance arrangements (such as partnerships) with statutory agencies will produce organisational development needs of yet a different order.

Whether a campaign, independent service provision, or co-governance is the organisational strategy of choice, issues relating to control over agendas and forms of decision making will require attention to 'first-' and 'second-face of power' issues as highlighted on pp 23–4.

6. Finally, *sustaining a community organisation and its strategy* will be another issue that will require addressing. This raises questions of continuation funding, empowerment orientated leadership (and/or management), organisational norms and operating systems, monitoring and organisational change management.

Conclusions

The argument in this chapter has been that a step-change in civic and political engagement by those at the 'sharp-end' of societal processes of disadvantage, exclusion and oppression is necessary. Such engagement entails working with power. Two basic models – power over and power with – have been identified and discussed, and the implications of these models for community empowerment strategies explored. It has been argued that while adoption of power-over strategies is generally seen to be 'what you do' in the contemporary context of working for social change, a strong case can be made for taking the more radical power-with option. Working within the power-with paradigm can be very effective in achieving longer-term, sustainable, change while at the same time challenging the ideological and structural hegemony of power-over practices. In Chapter Three the focus shifts from theory to practice, and some case examples of power-with community action initiatives are examined.

THREE

What is critical community practice?
Case studies and analysis

Hugh Butcher

Introduction

This chapter describes a number of concrete examples of critical community practice, along with an initial analysis of some of their common features. All of the examples chosen illustrate what, in the previous chapter, was called a 'power-with' approach to community empowerment, and the descriptive and analytical commentary on the case material at the end of the chapter provides a further basis on which to construct the model of critical community practice developed in Chapter Four.

First, however, and as an introduction to the case examples, it may be helpful to make explicit why the initiatives in this chapter deserve to be referred to as examples of '*critical* community practice'.

Critical community practice: some key features

Note at the outset that 'critical', in the present context, does not mean 'negative' or 'destructive'. On the contrary, adopting a 'critical' approach to community practice is put forward as a positive and forward-looking development, mirroring efforts made by practitioners in other practice fields to develop a critical approach to their particular fields of practice. (For references to such developments in the field of education see, for example, Darder et al (2003); for psychotherapy, Dryden and Feltham (1992); for social work, Healy (2000) and Fook (2002); and for law, Grigg-Spall (1992).)

With respect to community practice, a *critical* approach:

- involves an intellectually defensible, value-driven commitment to working *with* and *alongside* disadvantaged, excluded and oppressed communities, with the aim of supporting their efforts to address the disadvantage, exclusion and oppression that blight their lives: 'working with and alongside' entails the practitioner developing a dialogical and mutually aligned relationship between herself or himself and the community – working with, rather than working for, the community;
- acknowledges that the experience of poverty and oppression, at both individual and community levels, is shaped by deep-rooted sociopolitical and ideological processes embedded in society; critical community practice aims to support community action taken to challenge, and then modify, such sociopolitical and ideological dynamics;
- recognises that this wider societal context also helps to shape the nature, goals and impacts of community practice itself. Such an understanding prompts the practitioner to take a reflexive approach to their work, to remain vigilant to the possibility that their practice may, inadvertently, reinforce disadvantage, exclusion and oppression. This contradictory potential of community practice – to be potentially both an instrument of social control as well as an instrument of social emancipation – is acknowledged as something to be constantly aware of, and to be on guard against;
- entails working for *transformational* change. This is not to say that ameliorative change is valueless, but that substantial, long-term and sustainable reductions in disadvantage, exclusion and oppression can only be brought about by action directed at producing systemic changes at institutional levels. Critical community practice is committed, in other words, to working with communities to transform the macro-processes that construct and reproduce the domination and exploitation they experience;
- draws its intellectual inspiration and its drive for social-structural change from critical social theory. Such theory not only offers robust and convincing explanatory accounts of the kind of macro-processes alluded to above, it is also a kind of theory that offers clear signposts for transcending a fundamentally flawed 'present' in favour of a new, and more socially just, 'future'. Critical theory is, in other words, a theory that is both descriptive *and* emancipatory;
- rests on an acknowledgement, consistent with everything said so far, that social change is ubiquitous, continuous and 'normal', and that the critical practitioner is 'in the business' of positively engaging

with change processes at all levels, up to and including institutional levels;

- requires, finally, that the practitioner engage in a continuous process of review and reflection on the nature, direction and consequences of their involvement in action for change, both individually and as part of wider 'communities of practice' (Wenger, 1998). Practitioners become committed to engaging in processes of continuous self-reflection, action-learning and knowledge development designed to enhance their capacity for effective, relevant, value-driven practice within a changing environment.

In summary then, and to restate in a somewhat different way a conclusion reached at the end of Chapter Two, a critical approach to community practice demands that community practitioners 'raise their game' in three significant respects:

1. to engage in *critical theorising* to better understand how power dynamics in contemporary society generate and reproduce disadvantage, exclusion and oppression in communities, as well as to provide them with a perspective on how power can be used by communities to promote a more just and equal social order;
2. to engage with communities in *critical action* directed at transformational change;
3. to continuously hone and deploy their capacity as *critically reflective practitioners* – to advance their learning, and ultimately to improve their practice.

This way of framing our approach is heavily indebted to Ronald Barnett's influential account of the dimensions of 'critical being' (Barnett, 1997) with respect to higher education, and this summary deliberately makes use of his three-fold distinction between critical reflection, critical action and critical reason (what we call 'critical theorising'). In Chapter Four we draw further on Barnett's work in developing a provisional 'model of critical community practice'.

Case examples

We now turn to review a number of contemporary examples of critical community practice. The following case examples describe how communities have mobilised to exercise effective 'power with' through, in varying degrees, mobilising power at decisional, agenda setting, 'meaning-shaping', and discursive levels. The cases illustrate how community members have achieved, through joint action, 'agency' – developing 'power with' fuelled by an enhanced 'power within'.

Neighbourhood governance of schools in Chicago

(Details for this case study have been drawn from: Fung and Wright (2003); Moore and Merritt (2002); American Youth Policy Forum (1998).)

During the late 1980s, Chicago, the third largest city in the United States, embarked upon a programme of radical reform of the governance of its public school provision. During the previous decade the city's school system had come under increasing criticism from many quarters – parents, city business leaders, community members, and many others – for its failure to educate Chicago's children in acceptable ways and to acceptable standards. US Secretary of Education William Bennett called the Chicago public school system the 'worst in America' and the *Chicago Tribune* ran a series of articles in May 1988 which portrayed students and parents as 'victims of a highly centralised system, populated by bureaucrats more concerned about protecting their jobs than improving learning' (American Youth Policy Forum, 1998). This centralised school bureaucracy was perceived to be failing the schools on a massive scale. A community movement began to organise and campaign for change, ultimately managing to turn the top-heavy, hierarchical, educational bureaucracy on its head:

> In 1988 the Illinois legislature passed a law that decentralised and opened up governance of Chicago schools to direct forms of neighbourhood participation. The reform law shifted power and control from a centralised city-wide headquarters to the individual schools themselves. (Fung and Wright, 2003, p 7)

Each elementary school and high school (560 in all) became, under law, the responsibility of their own Local Schools Council (LSC) comprising six parents, two community members, two teachers, the school's principal, plus one non-voting student representative. The Councils met monthly. Only the principal served ex officio; all other members were elected to serve on the Council for a maximum term of two years. The Council became a powerful body:

> These councils are empowered, and required by law, to select principals, write principal performance contracts that they monitor and review every three years, develop annual

School Improvement Plans that address staff, program and infrastructure issues, monitor the implementation of those plans, and approve school budgets. (Fung and Wright, 2003, p 7)

Fung and Wright point out:

This reform created the most formally directly elected democratic system of school governance in the United States. Every year, more than five thousand parents, neighbourhood residents and school teachers are elected to run their schools. (2003, p 7)

Many of the schools flourished under their new governance regime. But some failed, partly through lack of skilled and competent people on the Council, partly through internal conflicts within the Council, and for other reasons, and the city authorities were forced to draw up revised regulations to address the problems. In 1995 legislation was passed requiring all Council members to undergo enhanced training on budgeting, principal selection, school improvement planning, group processes and other matters.

Chicago's LSCs have been the subject of two major research projects, summarised in 'Chicago's Local School Councils: What the Research Says'. The major conclusion, reached as a result of this research was:

The vast majority of LSCs are viable organisations that responsibly carry out their mandated duties and are active in building school–community partnerships. The initial worries that councils would infringe on professional autonomy have proved unfounded … we view the findings presented as largely validating the wisdom of the 1988 Reform Act. By devolving significant resources and authority to local school communities and by expanding opportunities for local participation by parents, community members, and staff, this reform has enlarged the capabilities of communities to solve local problems … The overall viability and accomplishment of Chicago's LSCs is clear cut … the issue is not whether they should exist, but how they can be strengthened. (Moore and Merritt, 2002, p 16)

Youth Councils: Espoo and Lambeth

(Details for this case study have been drawn from: London Borough of Lambeth (2006); Smith (2005); Rogers (2004) and personal communication with the author.)

Espoo is the second largest city in Finland, having grown rapidly during the 20th century owing to its expanding high-tech industrial base. The city is located in the south of the country, adjacent to the capital, Helsinki. In 1997 an independent Youth Council was established by young people in Espoo, and shortly afterwards the city's local governing board created a formal link with the Youth Council, allowing its members to sit on, and participate in the work of, the various city government committees. Youth Council members also have access to city offices and officials, liaise with local and national organisations, and act as the voice, and lobby on behalf, of youth in the city. Every autumn, members of the Council (comprising 15 males and 15 females – in 2005 the youngest was 13 years of age, the oldest 18 years of age) are elected by their peers, and hold office for a term of two years. Every Espoo resident between the ages of 13 and 18 has the right to cast their vote in the election. Voting takes place mainly in educational institutions – which has proved to be the best way to reach young people – but it is also possible to vote by post, internet or text message. In November 2005, 55 per cent of all students in Espoo voted in that year's annual Youth Council elections.

Proposals from young people are often generated and then discussed via an online 'Ideas Factory', the most popular of which, if feasible, are presented and discussed in the General Assembly of the Youth Council, which meets every three weeks. From here 'worked-up' proposals go to the city board or one of its sub-committees. Since 1997 about a quarter of all proposals generated in this way have eventually been enacted by the city board (Rogers, 2004, p 35).

The Finnish central government has recognised the success of Espoo and other pioneering Youth Councils, and has now set in place a system to roll out such Councils over the country as a whole. To date 80 have been established (Smith, 2005, p 60). The Finnish central government see the benefits of Youth Councils as threefold:

1. they provide young people with a voice, plus a mechanism, through which change can be achieved;
2. they provide effective citizenship education and encourage young people's future engagement in civic affairs and politics;

3. they foster the growth and development of the civic leaders of the future.

Lambeth, an inner-city borough in London, has also actively supported the development of its local Youth Council since its inception in 2002, although membership is not yet subject to the same democratic election process as in Espoo. Some 100 young people (aged between 11 and 24) have signed up to be members of the Council, and around 30 of them regularly attend the weekly meetings at Brixton Town Hall, taking turns as chair and actively moving a number of projects forward with the support of the Borough's Youth Development worker. The Youth Council decides on the initiatives to be taken up and these are run wholly by the members themselves; they include giving voice to the concerns of young people, seeking to influence policies that affect young people's lives, and initiating and running special projects. Recent initiatives include:

- An examination of the police's use of 'stop and search', a procedure of much concern to many young people in the community:

    The Youth Council interviewed key figures including the Chief Superintendent and the London Mayor's policy advisor on race. It subsequently provided feedback to the Home Office on new 'stop and search' guidelines and made presentations to the Lambeth Community Police Consultative Group and at a national conference. (Rogers, 2004, p 36)

    Youth Council members are now: 'developing materials and workshops to train police officers how to talk to young people properly when conducting stops and searches' (London Borough of Lambeth, Council website, 2006), and members have a role in training the police.
- The Youth Council's Teenage Pregnancy Project has involved members in drawing up model Personal, Social and Health Education lesson plans, aimed at conveying appropriate messages to reduce teenage pregnancy rates. These are used in school classroom sessions led by Youth Council Peer Educators in Lambeth's secondary schools, colleges and youth groups across the borough, following a six-week period of training.
- As part of the borough's quality control of its youth provision, Youth Council Peer Inspectors visit youth centres in all parts of Lambeth

to see that the way they are run conforms to the way young people would wish to see them run. A report and action plan are produced in conjunction with the Youth and Play Managers, and the Peer Inspectors revisit the youth centres at an agreed time to make sure recommendations have been implemented (London Borough of Lambeth, 2006).

The work of the Council is currently being extended across Lambeth; the plan being to establish a Youth Council in every town centre across the borough, and to train young people in the Youth Councils as video consultants – accessing the views of young people in their localities and feeding those views back to relevant decision-making bodies. Overall, young people involved in such initiatives have found them to constitute a profound experiential learning experience.

Cooperative community enterprise: Leicester and Minster

(Details for this case study have been drawn from: Cooperatives UK, 2006a; along with personal communications to the author.)

Leicester is the largest city in the East Midlands of England, and the tenth largest city in the country. It has a diverse population, the city's well-established ethnic minority community accounting for more than a third of Leicester's resident population. Somali Development Services (SDS) was established as a non-profit making cooperative (registered as a company limited by guarantee) in 2003, to assist in both addressing and coordinating the development needs of the small but growing Somali community in the city. Through their research, the SDS identified that the Somali community is one of the most disadvantaged in Leicester, and the cooperative set about tailoring its services to meet the most severe needs in the community:

> It offers educational and employment support and it is working with other key services to develop support in other areas including health and housing ... it is also running a range of projects including a homework club and outreach programme for young people, a family support service, drop-in sessions offering advice and information, and IT classes. (Cooperatives UK, 2006a)

The cooperative received its start-up capital from the East Midland Social Enterprise Development Fund, and it received in-depth help and advice from Voluntary Action Leicester, Community Action

Network, and the Leicester and County Cooperative Development Agency (LCCDA). It now has 16 women members, and an annual turnover of about £60,000. Members report that working for a community enterprise like SDS is rewarding on a number of levels – providing responsive and much needed services to members of their own community, through a cooperative form of organisation that instils a sense of ownership, and which is founded on principles of equality between members. At the same time it provides opportunities to learn new personal and relationship skills, as well as enhancing knowledge of project planning for community service delivery and raising levels of self-confidence and self-esteem.

The Minster Housing Cooperative was established in Swale District, north Kent, in 1999, to provide low-cost housing for people in priority need. It runs 36 properties, and the cooperative has 66 members (all tenants in the property it manages).

> Research by the Cooperative Development Agency (CDA) had revealed a need for social housing in Swale in Minster, Kent. They applied for a social housing grant to build 36 properties in the area in 1996 and then sought suitable tenants for the properties who became the initial members of the Minster Housing Cooperative. Three years later the ownership of the properties was transferred from CDA to the cooperative, after it had secured funding (a total of £1.2 million from the Housing Corporation and Nationwide Building Society) to purchase the houses collectively. (Cooperatives UK, 2006b)

The membership meets every four to six weeks to discuss general operational and developmental issues; and to receive reports from its committees. The members elect a 12-person management committee (11 are currently women), which is responsible for conducting the day-to-day business, for ensuring that the policies and procedures of the cooperative are implemented, and for overseeing finances (annual turnover is approximately £160,000). The wider goal of the cooperative is to develop a sustainable community, based on the strong relationships that have been nurtured between tenants living on the estate, and strengthened through the organisation of a range of community activities. The cooperative runs:

> a 'Kid's Club' which holds competitions, Christmas events, Easter egg competitions and sporting events for children

living within the cooperative estate, and it plans to introduce the children to cooperative principles as they get older ... By working together under the structure of a cooperative the tenant members have created a strong sense of community and collective responsibility. (Cooperatives UK, 2006b)

Local participatory budgeting: Port Alegre and Salford/Harrow

(Details for this case study have been drawn from: Abers (1996); London Borough of Harrow (2006); Salford City Council (2006); SQW (2006); World Bank (2006); Smith (2005); and Learner and Schugurensky (2005).)
Since 1989, the Brazilian city of Port Alegre has been engaged in an experiment in participatory governance that has excited interest across the world. Attempts to broaden and deepen civic governance, building upon the Port Alegre example, are to be found in other Brazilian cities, in cities in other Latin American countries as well as in Europe; in the UK experiments are under way in Salford (Salford City Council, 2006) and Harrow (London Borough of Harrow, 2006), among other cities. To date, none of these UK examples have gone as far as the Port Alegre experiment in achieving the breadth and depth of directly democratic and deliberative approaches to public budgeting.

During the 1970s and 1980s the Union of Neighbourhood Associations in Port Alegre had been increasing its demands for more democratic city government, and in 1984 its Congress called for the introduction of a participatory approach to determining the municipal budget. When the Popular Front – a broad-based electoral alliance, headed by the Workers Party (*Pardido dos Trabalhandos*, PT) – achieved victory in the 1989 city elections it set about responding to the Congress's resolution by extending an element of popular control over the municipal budgeting process. This was no easy task in a regional capital serving a relatively wealthy metropolitan area of three million people and in which, although overall socioeconomic conditions were above the national average (for example, life expectancy was over 70 years, literacy rates exceeded 90 per cent), there were also high levels of poverty, slum housing, urban degradation and other indicators of disadvantage and social exclusion.

The 'participatory budgeting' process in Port Alegre (*Orcamento particitivo*) introduced a two-tier structure of citizen-fora through which the population, in increasing numbers from 1989 onwards, has participated both as individuals and as representatives of civil society groups and organisations (neighbourhood associations, special interest groups, and cultural groups, for example), in plenary and district meetings to plan the annual city budget. The budgetary cycle begins in March, with a first round of 16 city-district assemblies. Up to 1,000 people attend these meetings which, with the mayor and senior city executives in attendance, conducts a review of the previous year's programmes and projects, and elects delegates to represent specific neighbourhoods in successive rounds of deliberation on the following year's budget. Elected delegates also meet to:

- learn about the technical details of project and programme budgeting;
- engage in intensive open meetings in their own districts to deliberate local priority needs;
- work with their fellow delegates to discuss and make decisions about programmes that will affect the city as a whole over and above those that concern specific neighbourhoods. Thematic assemblies are also formed to work on specific policy areas like health and education.

These rounds of meetings end with a second plenary meeting, when delegates vote to ratify the district's priorities as well as elect councillors to serve on the Municipal Council of the Budget whose main function is to reconcile district demands and to approve the Municipal Budget.

In Port Alegre the proportion of the city budget controlled through these exercises in direct participation has risen from 2 per cent in 1989 to nearly 20 per cent currently.

Research interest in the Port Alegre experiment (concerning its process and its outcomes) has been extensive (see for example, World Bank, 2001, 2006; Schugurensky, 2004). In terms of 'process', findings include:

- Participatory budgeting has encouraged increasing levels of local political engagement; involvement of around 1,000 citizens in 1990 had risen to 40,000 by 1999. It has been described as 'a school of Citizenship' – citizens learn democracy by doing, acquiring 'a great variety' of political skills, knowledge, attitudes and values. Self-esteem increases, as well as participants' sense of political efficacy (Schugurensky, 2004).
- A secondary effect has been a growth in neighbourhood and community associations (from 300 in 1989 to 540 in 1998), as well as growth in other forms of civil society organisations (for example, the number of cooperatives increased from 11 in 1989 to 51 in 1998).

- In terms of the social background of those who become actively involved, it has been found that 'better-off' citizens are *under*-represented, while those on lower incomes and poorer levels of education are *over*-represented.

Turning to substantive outcomes, UN and other reports attribute the following changes largely to the introduction of participatory budgeting (UN, 2004; and see World Bank 2001, 2006):

- Provision of new housing units increased from 500 to 1,000 per annum during the period 1989–2003.
- The percentage of dwellings with access to the municipal sewer network rose from 46 per cent to 89 per cent over the period 1987–2002.
- In terms of education, the number of public schools rose from 29 to 88 (1987–2002), with a corresponding increase in enrolments from 18,000 to 54,000 students.
- The city health and education budget grew from 13 per cent of the total budget to nearly 40 per cent between 1987 and 1996.
- There has been a 50 per cent increase in tax revenues since the introduction of participatory budgeting (as a result of increased transparency in tax rates, and payments received – which has encouraged payment of taxes).

Over the recent past significant interest in participatory budgeting has grown in the UK and across Europe. In 2002 Salford City Council embarked upon a pilot study (Salford City Council, 2006), and in 2005 the London Borough of Harrow began piloting a participatory budget process (London Borough of Harrow, 2006). Both the Salford and Harrow initiatives are still in the early stages of development, and are still evolving, using different methods. The approaches adopted are, at present, best seen as exercises in community consultation rather than co-governance. However, an independent consultancy report which compared the approaches in Salford and Harrow noted that participants generally reported themselves very satisfied with the process and welcomed the opportunity to be consulted in a meaningful way (SQW, 2006).

Reflections on the case examples

So, what tentative conclusions can be drawn from these case example, in terms of both their practical feasibility and their potential benefits? The word 'tentative' is used advisedly. We have provided examples of only a limited number of initiatives, very different in their scale, approach and focus, and undertaken in widely different social contexts. Furthermore, they have been chosen purposefully (to illustrate our arguments) rather than randomly (to test our arguments).

They should best be thought of as 'prefigurative' of wider transformatory social change. Such initiatives draw their inspiration from models of democratic participation, social citizenship, governance, power and social change that challenge prevailing mindsets and values underpinning many mainstream institutions and social practices. At best, all they can do is to provide us with a kind of 'reality check', a crude litmus test of how far advocacy of critical community practice can be regarded as something more than an exercise in utopian speculation, and that it can be taken seriously as a realistic approach to community change.

With these caveats in mind we present our reflections under two broad headings: reflections on the processes illustrated in the case examples, and reflections on the outcomes achieved by the initiatives.

Reflections on process

- *Participatory governance:* The case examples illustrate that workable and effective participatory governance underpinned by democratic principles can be devised which is capable of augmenting the practices of conventional representative democracy. Public expenditure budgeting, school governance, cooperative-based approaches to running community services and young people's engagement in local government decision making have all been shown to be susceptible to an element of direct democratic influence or control by ordinary members of local communities. The forms of direct governance illustrated in the case examples were more participative (wider) and more dialogical (deeper) than is conventionally found in local democratic systems, and arguably the level of engagement was more authentic and less superficial and tokenistic than many other contemporary exercises in 'citizen involvement and participation'. The case examples also illustrate how the community members involved in these governance activities became actively engaged with all three 'faces' of power; helping to re-frame solutions to community problems, turning those solutions into proposals for democratic public consideration, and then taking decisions for action that 'made a difference' to the quality of important aspects of their lives. It is also worth noting that in all the case studies reported here aspects of leadership were shared. There was little evidence of leadership functions being concentrated in any one person with particular charisma or influence. Leadership of particular tasks and functions tended to be distributed around those involved according to interests and expertise. Finally the case examples challenge an often heard objection to participatory forms of governance – that it is fundamentally unworkable in complex modern societies with their mobile populations, fragmented communities, and their reliance on specialist expertise (political, professional and administrative) to formulate, implement and monitor policies effectively. The case examples do, at the very least, show that an interest in direct forms of democracy need not be limited to historical study of the Greek city state and the 18th-century New England town meeting.

- *Active citizenship:* Participatory governance can make heavy demands on the citizen – some say too heavy for the majority of citizens in modern society to want to bear. However, our case examples show that significant numbers of citizens, given the opportunity for involvement within a carefully structured institutional framework that is seen to be fair and effective, are willing to devote much time and effort to public affairs, not only from a self-interested point of view, but also from the point of view of contributing to the public good. While some commentators bewail the growth of the privatised citizen, as irredeemably 'consumerist' and 'individualist' in their perspective, content to limit their political engagement to voting (in decreasing numbers, and with diminishing interest) for the representative most likely to 'get on with job' of looking after their interests, we see that 40,000 citizens in Port Alegre actively engaged in the politics and administration of local public expenditure, that in Chicago 5,000 parents and residents were elected to run their schools, and in Espoo 55 per cent of all students voted in the Annual Youth Council elections.

    Moreover such active engagement is not limited to the more educated and better-off sections of the community – indeed, there was a tendency for such sections of the community to be *under-represented*; the disadvantaged and less educated were *over-represented* in our examples.

    Further, the examples indicated that ordinary people *are* capable of drawing up policies and plans, and running services and programmes in a responsible and effective manner. The Somali People's Centre set up and ran a series of services responsive to the needs of their highly disadvantaged community; members of the Lambeth Youth Council were active in developing training materials that have been adopted by the local police service; and, in Chicago, LSCs have drawn up, and then monitored, the implementation of school improvement plans.

The case examples also show that such engagement, though demanding, can be both rewarding and educational to participants. Members of the Minster Housing Association and the Somali People's Centre commented on how rewarding their engagement with a cooperative form of organisation had been, based as it was on values of community, collective responsibility and equality between members. The Chicago LSCs enlarged citizens' capabilities in community problem solving, and the Espoo Youth Council provided a rich form of citizenship education and helped foster the growth and development of the civic leaders of the future. All the case examples indicated that participants found their involvement a fulfilling action-learning experience.

- *Working across boundaries:* Each of the case studies illustrate the importance of working with a range of interrelated organisational systems. This is partly an inevitable consequence of adopting a 'power-with' approach, but it is also partly because the interests and objectives of community members can rarely be addressed by any one agency operating alone, within the confines of its own organisational 'silo'. The Espoo Youth Council, for example, made it its business to engage with a number of City Board Committees, and in Lambeth the Youth Council engaged with the local police and educational services, the Home Office, and the Office of the Mayor of London in order to advance the cause of young people in the borough. In Chicago, the LSCs entered into community partnerships, as well as working with teacher organisations and with City Hall; and the cooperative enterprises reported on here worked closely with a range of statutory and voluntary sector organisations, including development agencies, building societies and funding bodies. Critical community practice entails, then, that communities and their organisations work in and through the wider system of, for example, state and not-for-profit organisations, professional organisations and trade unions, and social movement bodies, as well as other neighbourhood and community groups.

- *Institutional supports:* The case examples point to the importance of building accountable and popular institutional structures if experiments in participatory governance, underpinned by the engagement of an active citizenry, are to become effective and sustainable. All of these experiments required much time and effort, over years rather than months, in order to become robust and durable elements of their local power structures. In each case new governance structures had to overcome setbacks and difficulties; some of Chicago's LSCs failed initially, and operational systems had to be rethought and revised in order to overcome unproductive cleavages and internal conflict undermining effective operations. In Port Alegre participatory budgeting evolved from modest origins, and much hard work was necessary to establish workable and agreed rules for moderating the deliberative aspect of participatory governance.

A further common feature revealed by the case examples was the importance of establishing enabling support structures for participants. In the locally based cooperatives in Swale and Leicester the support roles played by such bodies as the Cooperative Development Agency and the Cooperative Support Fund were vital. In Port Alegre delegates attended teach-ins on the technical aspects of programme budgeting as well as workshops on group process for effective group and committee work. All members of the Chicago LSCs received training on such topics as principal selection, school improvement processes and school budgeting.

Reflections on outcomes

From our case examples there is evidence that participatory governance can contribute to realising the following kinds of outcomes:

- Improvements in the *quality* of community services (for example, schooling in Chicago, policing in Lambeth);
- Improvements in the *quantity* of community services (for example, social housing in Swale; family support, employment and educational advice services to an ethnic minority community in Leicester);
- Innovations in the *form* of existing service provision (for example, youth pregnancy services in Lambeth);
- *Community* and *social-capital development* (in Swale, for example, the activities of the Minster Housing Association helped to strengthen community identity and a sense of collective responsibility. In Port Alegre the significant growth in neighbourhood and community associations, as well as growth in other civil society organisations, has been attributed, at least in part, to the introduction of the

participatory budgeting process. There is also some evidence to show that such initiatives generate community solidarity and an enhanced concern for aspects of wider 'common goods' over advocacy of individual or group self-interest. And all of the initiatives have acted as a forcing ground for citizenship learning – including political skills and knowledge – and have increased participants' sense of self-esteem and civic efficacy);

- *Redistributive effects* – finally, there are indications that some of the initiatives have been instrumental in bringing about some redistribution of public goods (for example, in Port Alegre the proportion of the city budget allocated to health and educational services has increased substantially, and there is evidence that disadvantaged groups have benefited over wealthier population segments).

Conclusions

This chapter has offered both a general and a specific answer to the question, 'What is critical community practice?'. At the general level we have seen that critical community practice can be seen to be about communities of the disadvantaged, excluded and oppressed working in an empowered way to assist them in their efforts to achieve social justice through transformatory change in society.

Empowerment has been used as a key idea in this chapter and we have sought to illustrate dimensions of the concept (as highlighted in Chapter Two) via an analysis of power in a number of different social contexts. In focusing on the dynamics of power, our understanding of critical community practice is consistent with other attempts to theorise critical forms of social practice.

Our more specific answer has entailed an emphasis on 'power-with' (non zero-sum) definitions of power, as a result of our attempt to deploy a power analysis to introduce greater rigour to the use of the term 'empowerment'. At the same time, and following from our primary interest in community power, our approach to critical community practice has focused on the transformative potential of new forms of local democratic governance (both more participative and deliberative), in public and civil society, as a means to changing those social conditions that construct disadvantaged, excluded and oppressed communities. The case studies have been used to illustrate, in a prefigurative manner, what some of the outputs and broader outcomes of utilising such an approach might be.

We now turn from this focus on critical community practice as a particular kind of change process – concerned with new forms of power relations, citizen involvement and community governance – to focus, in Chapter Four, on what *doing* critical community practice entails, directing our attention to the values, mindset, skills and activities required of those who work (at grass-roots, organisational, policy or political levels) with such change processes.

FOUR

Towards a model of critical community practice

Hugh Butcher

Introduction

This chapter builds on the analysis offered in the previous chapters, in order to construct a working model of critical community practice. The model seeks to provide a cogent, coherent and comprehensive approach to theorising, implementing and reflecting upon such practice. The model is presented in diagrammatic form in Figure 4.1 and comprises four interlocking components:

1. a specification of the characteristics of a distinctively critical approach to practical social and community *action*;
2. an outline of a robust framework for *theorising* such practice;
3. the case for a form of *reflection* and reflexivity capable of questioning, supporting and reviewing such practice and theory;
4. articulation of the presuppositions underpinning what we call '*critical consciousness*' – the assumptions, values and dispositions on which the model derives its potential appeal and vitality.

Figure 4.1: Community critical practice – a model

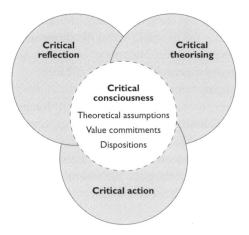

In what follows, each of these elements is elaborated in turn, and some of the key interconnections between them are drawn out.

In order to illustrate the model in concrete terms we return to the examples of critical community practice presented in Chapter Three, drawing upon the generalisations we formulated at the end of that chapter about the processes and outcomes that characterised these initiatives. Those case examples were all representative of the 'radical democracy' perspective. We believe that this model has wider applicability and, space permitting, could have been illustrated from initiatives shaped by anti-racist, feminist, green, alternative economic, and other radical paradigms. Readers are invited to examine the model in terms of one or more of these alternative radical frameworks, not least those that inform their own practice.

Use of the terms 'community practice' and 'community practitioner' was explained in the Introduction to this book and it is important to reiterate, in the context of the present chapter, that 'community practice' is not seen here as the preserve of any one occupational or functional group in society. A wide range of occupations, social groups and organisational actors have roles to play in progressing community practice: political and other policy makers, managers of public and not-for-profit sector organisations, a wide range of professional workers, as well as citizens actively working for community change. They all play roles in stimulating and strengthening commitment to such practice. Equally, they all have a role to play in progressing *critical* community practice. For some, the role and its associated activities will be a central part of their life and work; for others, such roles and activities will be more peripheral, or only central during a particular phase of their life or career. We return to examine the particular roles played by these key players later in this chapter.

We will have met our objectives if the model:

1. offers a framework through which key concerns touched on in previous chapters – for example social disadvantage, exclusion and oppression, power and empowerment – can be considered and addressed in an appropriately integrated fashion;
2. provides a basis on which the chapters that follow can explore particular aspects of practice in more depth, for example policy and politics, organisational management, supervision of critical community practice;
3. stimulates, as well as provides a potential basis on which to pursue, further discussions about the need for, and role of, *critical* approaches to community practice.

Critical consciousness

The term chosen to summarise the central element in the model
– 'critical consciousness' – is most famously associated with the
writings of the 20th-century political activist Antonio Gramsci (1971)
who coined the term, and more particularly for current purposes, the
work of the Brazilian educator Paulo Freire (1972). Freire's model of
'problem-posing' adult learning has been widely adopted by community
practitioners in Africa as well other Latin American countries, and has
been deployed by some community practitioners in the industrialised
countries of the northern hemisphere. Freire used dialogical methods
of action-learning in his literacy development work with impoverished
agricultural workers as a vehicle for raising critical awareness about
the way disadvantage and oppression, and a denial of personal and
collective agency, had been imposed upon the peasant workers and
was maintained through dominant social institutions and ideologies.
'Conscientisation' generated the energy, hope and knowledge base on
which to pursue 'action for liberation'.

Although the use of the term 'critical consciousness' here does not
mirror Freire's concept of 'conscientisation' exactly, the model of critical
community practice advanced here has been much influenced by his
work, and the adoption of his terminology is testament to the influence
of his thought. In our model, 'critical consciousness' is seen to embrace
a set of theoretical assumptions, a commitment to social justice, and a
particular set of dispositions on the part of the practitioner. In addition
to Freire, the 'critical consciousness' component of the model draws
on the work of a number of other thinkers – most notably Jürgen
Habermas (1975, 1996), but also John Dewey (1986 [1910]), Stephen
Brookfield (1987, 2005), John Chaffee (1998), Peter Vaill (1996) and
others – although it should be noted that many of these authors are
also indebted to Freire as a major influence on their own writing.

Theoretical assumptions

Critical community practice is grounded in the following assumptions
about the nature of human beings, community and society:

1. *Human sociality:* Human beings are regarded first and foremost as
   social animals, dependent on other human beings for a wide range
   of biological, emotional and cognitive needs. There is considerable
   sociological and social-psychological evidence to show that the
   process of personality formation and growth is dependent in large

measure on social interaction. Studies of feral children, for example, suggest that a human baby, left without human interaction, will never become much more than a helpless animal (Olsen, 1970, p 24; Stark, 1996, pp 151–2).

So our first assumption is that human beings are, collectively, 'interdependent', one with another, and that their 'human' nature necessarily arises as a social product, shaped as a consequence of living in a particular kind of society. Benjamin Barber neatly brings out the implication of this assumption for an understanding of both 'community' and 'citizenship':

> If we accept the postulate that humans are social by nature, then we cannot regard citizenship as merely one among many artificial social roles that can be grafted onto man's natural solitariness. It is rather the only legitimate form that man's natural dependency can take. The civic bond is the sole legitimator of the indissoluble natural bond; it makes *voluntary* those ties that cannot in any case be undone, and it makes *common* and susceptible to mutuality the fate that is in any case shared by all men. (Barber, 1984, p 217)

2. *Symbolisation and symbolic communication:* Secondly, critical community practice rests on an assumption that human beings have a high-level capacity for symbolisation and symbolic communication – that they can and do have a capacity to think and communicate using abstract symbols, which is far in advance of all other species. Many argue that such a capacity is unique in its scope and importance for shaping contemporary human social existence. While examples can be found of species that clearly have an organised collective life (ants and bees, for example), such life is nevertheless primarily determined by instinctive behaviour. Almost all significant human action and (collective) social life involves symbol manipulation and communication and it is this which enables humans to relate to each other in voluntaristic and purposive ways. As humans we orientate our actions to take into account what (we believe) others are thinking and feeling and how this influences what we observe of their behaviour. We thus have the capacity to modify our own thoughts and actions as a consequence of what we believe or discover about others' thinking and feelings. Further, humans' ability to use and manipulate abstract symbols endows them with the capacity for rational thought, reflection and imagination.

The assumption, then, is that human beings collectively *create,* through symbolisation and communication, the network of social relationships and social institutions that comprise their collective life, as well as jointly *construct* the complex of artefacts, beliefs, norms, values and theories that is called *culture.* Social and cultural integration is achieved in and through symbolic communication and, as noted above, values and beliefs are similarly 'constructed' in concert with others.

3. *Society and social institutions as socially constructed:* It follows that this capacity for voluntaristic and purposive interaction, along with the capacity for rational thought, reflection and imagination (Assumption 2), when allied with the assumption that human beings are 'collectively interdependent' (Assumption 1) provides human beings with the ability to accomplish the task of jointly designing and constructing (and reconstructing) aspects of their social relationships and social institutions.

   This third assumption underpinning critical community practice is, then, that human beings possess the potential to jointly develop and shape patterns of social relationships and social institutions in a considered and potentially rational manner – including those social and institutional structures that provide a (democratic) basis for determining a shared life in society.

4. *Human beings as socially constituted:* However, for any particular 'individual' in society, community and culture 'pre-exist', and confront, them as a social fact. As their developing capacity for symbolisation and communications is shaped via socialisation into a particular language, and as specific patterns of social relationships and institutional structures come to be taken for granted (as 'the way things are'), so they become 'constituted' by the communities of which they are a part. This assumption distances us from the philosophical view (sometimes referred to as 'social atomism') that individuals, as it were, come together *instrumentally* to 'form' their communities and societies and that the individual subject is to be thought of as logically, and ontologically, prior to social, political and ethical reality (Taylor, 1985, pp 187–210). Furthermore, it also supports the view that 'society' is experienced as an emergent reality, and that the 'social system' is experienced as a constraining 'fact'.

   This fourth assumption then (taken together with the second one) means that the model of critical community practice presented here rests on a version of that system of thought called philosophical communitarianism (Frazer, 1999). Critical community practice is based on a theoretical approach that gives primacy to the intersubjective dimensions of social reality. Community is neither to be thought of as an aggregate of discrete 'pre-social' individuals who 'decide' to band together in a social unit for purely instrumental reasons, nor is it to be thought of as an organic unity in which the constituent individuals are totally subservient 'creatures' of the whole. It is, rather, to be conceived of as an 'open' system that changes and evolves in response to its external environment, as well as internally to the collective actions of its members.

5. *Democratic decision making:* The final working assumption holds that deliberative and participatory models of democracy become available as approaches to collective decision making in communities as a consequence of the previous four assumptions. If all members of a community have an equal stake and ownership of it, share the life and opportunities offered by communal living ('mutual interdependence'), and have the capacity to engage in discussion about its future, then it can argued that there is no reasonable justification for not giving due consideration to the views of all. To do otherwise is to treat some as means to others' ends, so diminishing or negating their 'personhood', and thus acting oppressively.

Value commitments

In previous chapters reference has been made to a range of value commitments that inform and underpin critical community practice. In Chapter Two, for example, it was noted that a commitment to *social justice* (including promoting equality and fairness, as well as a respect for social difference) was integral to critical community practice in its attempt to overcome disadvantage, exclusion and oppression. A commitment to the value of *self-determination* (both collective and individual) led us to emphasise the importance of citizens taking more control over the conditions of their lives by securing greater levels of civic and political engagement in democratic processes. In Chapter Three emphasis was again given to the importance of social values when discussing the importance that critical community practice puts on reshaping the social, political and ideological dynamics of contemporary society. That chapter also discussed the question of practitioners' action principles – the value placed on dialogical and enabling working practices, of 'power-with' and partnership working, of educational processes and conscientisation.

In the present context it is helpful in discussing values to distinguish between ideals, principles of action, and desirable outcomes. Ideals comprise the central 'core' principles and values regarded as desirable and worthwhile 'in themselves', and these are usually expressed in fairly general – even abstract – terms, as ideals towards which personal, organisational and political action should be orientated. Principles of action guide choices about the best (or preferred) ways of achieving such ideals; if ideals determine 'destinations', principles of action shape the 'journey' taken to reach them. Finally, in taking personal, organisational and political action, ideals and principles of action are intended to lead to the achievement of desirable outcomes, short term and long term, specific and general. Drawing on these conceptual distinctions enables a provisional list of the key normative beliefs pursued by critical community practitioners to be drawn up as follows.

Ideals of critical community practice comprise:

- *social justice* – a commitment to a fairer and more equal distribution of resources, power, and life chances in society;
- *social inclusion* – a recognition of, and respect for, social diversity, along with the eradication of demeaning and oppressive behaviour, relationships and practices;
- *social self-determination* – a commitment to maximising opportunities for people to determine the conditions (social, community, organisational, political) of their own lives;
- *social solidarity* – a positive value placed on cooperative, collaborative, social action – both in recognition of human sociality, and as a corrective to an over-emphasis on atomistic and egoistic assumptions as the mainsprings of human social action.

Principles of action of critical community practice comprise:

- *conscientisation* – the development, through action for change, of a particular form of critical consciousness, which generates the hope, energy and know-how necessary to achieve 'action for liberation';
- *empowerment* – the collective mobilisation of power to shape public decisions, influence agendas, and effectively challenge hegemonic ideologies and oppressive discourses;
- *collective action* – the development of the motivation, skills and capacities to work cooperatively with others to effect change through active citizenship.

Desirable outcomes of critical community practice comprise:

- *transformational change* in societal institutions – through conscientisation, empowerment and collective action – driven on by the ideals of social justice, inclusivity, self-determination and solidarity outlined above;
- *emancipation* of individuals and groups from disadvantage, exclusion and oppression through citizen action within participatory and deliberative democracy.

While it may be helpful to differentiate the normative beliefs of critical community practice in this way, it is important to note that such a listing does not imply a 'hierarchy' of values. There has been a long-running debate among community practitioners about the relative emphasis given to the value of 'process goals' and 'end-state goals/outcomes'. Is community practice primarily about 'enabling' and 'empowering' communities to determine their *own* goals and strengthen their capacity to realise them? Or is it primarily about working with communities to achieve *publicly sanctioned* goals that, through a society's due democratic processes, have been judged to be consistent with that society's conception of the public interest? Critical community practice finds this distinction unhelpful. If critical community practice is about promoting awareness of the way social processes that produce social disadvantage and oppression can be 'other than they are', and is about empowering citizens to take action to broaden and deepen the democratic processes through which the desirable outcomes of community, organisational and political change can be realised, then both the practices and the goals of critical community practice are consistent with the public interest in 'actually existing' as well as 'aspiring' democratic practices.

Dispositions

The title of Peter Vaill's book *Learning as a way of being* (1996) neatly captures the third element of critical consciousness to be discussed here. The central message of Vaill's book is that contemporary life is akin to navigating a boat through the turbulence and hazards of permanent 'white-water' rapids. Permanent white water is full of surprises, producing problems of navigation that are novel, ill defined and challenging. To navigate such waters skilfully requires individuals to integrate the disciplines of learning into their very being, to adopt learning, as Vaill says, 'as a whole mentality':

> It is more than a skill, learning as a way of being is a
> whole posture towards experience, a way of framing and
> interpreting all experience as a learning opportunity or
> learning process. (Vaill, 1996, p 51)

Permanent white water as a metaphor for complex, rapid and
discontinuous social (and organisational) change, as well as an injunction
to embrace learning as 'a way of being' as a necessary response, is
particularly relevant to the critical community practitioner. Such
practitioners are, after all, not only working *within* an environment
of 'white water change'; their values, working assumptions and
commitment to change impel them to act as a prime mover in ways
that significantly *add* to such change! For them, learning – more
specifically learning in and through action – as a way of being provides
critical community practice with its key dynamic: learning results
from continuously reviewing and reflecting on the model in use, to
keep on questioning and reviewing the formulation of its guiding
value commitments and its theoretical assumptions in the light of new
knowledge from experience and from developments in theory. For the
critical community practitioner to adopt 'action-learning as a way of
being' entails the following:

**Action-learning as a way of being: learning to reason, evaluate, take
account of evidence, and exercise creative thought:** The importance of
critical thinking skills has, of course, long been recognised within both
academe and practical life as a vital life skill. In *The thinker's way* John
Chaffee notes that:

> The word *critical* comes from the Greek word 'critic' (*kriticos*),
> meaning to question, to make sense of, to analyse. It is by
> questioning, making sense of and analysing that you examine
> your thinking and the thinking of others. These critical
> activities aid us in reaching the best possible conclusions and
> decisions. The word *critical* is also related to the word *criticise*,
> which means to question and evaluate. Unfortunately the
> ability to criticise is often used destructively, to tear down
> someone else's thinking. Criticism, however, can also be
> *constructive* – analysing for the purpose of developing a
> better understanding of what is going on. (Chaffee, 1998,
> pp 34–5)

In critical community practice practitioners necessarily engage in constructive criticism as they exercise and develop their critical capacities. Chaffee argues that 'becoming a critical thinker is a total approach to the way we understand our world' (1998, p 35), and involves an integrated set of thinking abilities that include the following:

- *an ability to analyse and evaluate your own beliefs* in order to develop the most accurate beliefs possible;
- *an ability to view situations from different perspectives* in order to develop in-depth understanding;
- *a willingness to support viewpoints with reasons and evidence* in order to arrive at thoughtful, well-substantiated conclusions;
- *a capacity to critically appraise the personal 'lenses'* that shape and influence the way we perceive the world;
- *a skilfulness in synthesising information* in order to reach informed conclusions.

In *Developing critical thinkers* (1987) Stephen Brookfield takes the position developed by Chaffee a step further, showing the importance of critical thinking to the practice of informal education in the community. This application is of particular interest, as community education is an important part of community practice.

Action-learning as a way of being: the importance of emotional intelligence: Critical consciousness is not just about the practitioner's capacity to reason, to weigh evidence, to use logic, and to deploy thinking skills in as rigorous and purposive a way as possible. It is also about recognising, respecting and using feelings – to acknowledge, for example, the hurt, abhorrence and outrage at the disadvantages, exclusions and oppressions that result from inequality and injustice. Action-learning as a way of being entails developing and using emotional intelligence (Goleman, 1995) in a way that develops one's capacity to accurately perceive and manage emotions; to harness emotions to facilitate thinking; and to use emotions to motivate and fuel effective action (Salovey and Mayer, 1990). As we shall see, emotional intelligence is key to effective reflection and, as Dewey acknowledges, critical thinking itself has both emotional and intellectual components. It entails the intellectual and emotional strength to go beyond the known 'without falling to pieces'.

Action-learning as a way of being; learning as dialogical: In *Words and minds* Neil Mercer (2000) discusses how people learn (and think about things critically) *together.* He shows how 'we use our language to think together, for collectively making sense of experience and solving problems' (Mercer, 2000, p 1). He argues that we do this 'inter-thinking' in ways that most of us take for granted but which is at the heart of human achievement. His work is particularly useful to the community practitioner in that it directly relates to the position put forward here – that processes of dialogue and deliberation are central to the transformatory ambitions of critical practice. As noted, Freire emphasised the importance of dialogue (cooperative critical interrogation of lived experience among groups of people, founded on equality and mutual respect) as a basis for awareness-raising and practical action. Much community practice entails group work, teamwork, community co-partnerships and so on, and a critical approach to such activity needs to take on board the importance of establishing guidelines for facilitating the productivity and democratisation of such 'interthinking' in community contexts.

Action-learning as a way of being: organisational and societal learning: It is only a modest step from the idea of 'inter-thinking' to developing workable concepts about organisational learning, and the learning society. Strictly speaking, only people are capable of learning, but Salomon makes the useful distinction between a 'person-solo' who learns, and a 'person plus' who learns with others:

> People appear to think in conjunction or partnership with others and with the help of culturally provided tools and implements. Cognitions, it would seem, are not content-free tools that are brought to bear on this or that problem; rather, they emerge in a situation tackled by teams of people and the tools available to them ... What characterises such daily events of thinking is that the social and artifactual surrounds, alleged to be 'outside' the individual's heads, not only are sources of stimulation and guidance but are actually vehicles of thought. Moreover, the arrangements, functions, and structures of these surrounds change in the process to become genuine parts of learning that result from cognitive partnership with them. Thus it is not just the 'person-solo' who learns, but the 'person-plus', the whole system of interrelated factors. (Salomon, 1993, p xiii)

Theorists of organisational learning have focused on how this 'whole system of interrelated factors' can be best developed to enhance learning in organisational contexts, and Butcher and Robertson have enumerated some of these under the headings of organisational culture, organisational processes and organisational structures in their discussion of 'Individual and organisational development for community practice' (Butcher and Robertson, 2003, p 97).

In his book *The fifth discipline*, Peter Senge (1990) similarly argues that a 'learning organisation' is more than an organisation whose members are committed to (and receive support to achieve) continuous individual learning. Rather it is one in which learning takes place and is resourced to happen at the collective level; it is one in which action-learning is woven into the very fabric of the organisation.

Policy makers concerned with designing the organisational architecture through which community practice can be properly supported and managers concerned with leading and running such organisations will find much of relevance in the theory and practice of organisational learning. We explore these themes further in Chapter Five.

Critical consciousness: concluding comments

It has been argued that 'critical consciousness' provides the foundation on which all aspects of critical community practice rest. It comprises a disposition and mindset that entails community practitioners working to enhance their critical and creative capacities, their enquiry and analytical skills, and their powers of reflection, both as individuals and in concert with others. These critical capacities inform the theory that practitioners deploy, the action they take, and the reflection and learning that constitute an integral part of their practice. But most importantly, critical consciousness is used to continuously review ideals, assumptions and dispositions in order that, in a reflexive way, they further develop their effectiveness in their chosen field of practice.

Critical theorising

As already noted, Barnett (1997) characterises critical theory as a type of social theory that not only provides an understanding of present-day social relationships and institutions, but also makes us aware of how such relationships and institutions can be other than they are. In elaborating the 'critical theorising' component of the model we will draw upon radical democratic theory as an example of such theory, showing how the idea of 'participatory community governance' can help us to envision how social relationships and institutions can be 'other than they are'.

Some problems with 'actually existing' democracy

Advocacy of radical democracy (including its participatory and deliberative variants) has re-emerged as a powerful force for change during the past 20 years, as a response to increasing dissatisfaction with existing forms of liberal social democracy (Barber, 1984; Habermas, 1975, 1996; Fung and Wright, 2003).

Why the dissatisfaction? In their recent report, members of the Power Inquiry (2006) reviewed the range of reasons advanced for what they called the 'problem of democratic disengagement', concluding that the best evidence supports the following explanations:

- Citizens do not feel the democratic process offers them enough influence over decisions that determine the conditions of their lives.
- The main political parties are perceived to lack principles.
- The main political parties are too similar in their prescriptions and policies.
- Voting procedures are seen as inconvenient and unattractive, and besides, the electoral system is seen to lead to wasted votes.
- People feel they lack knowledge and information on which to engage in politics. (Power Inquiry, 2006, p 17)

Further, the authors of the report argue that such dissatisfactions are becoming ever stronger, driven by the consequential effects of a progressively more educated citizenry that expects to take more control over more aspects of their lives, and whose members are less and less inclined to be deferential to those in authority. This analysis certainly echoes our reflections on the case exemplars in Chapter Three, as does a further set of factors to which the Inquiry draws attention:

> ... the creation of permanently marginalised groups in society which live in persistent poverty, with low educational attainment, poor working and living conditions and a multiplicity of other deprivations associated with life on low or very low incomes. (Power Inquiry, 2006, p 18)

The theory of participative and deliberative democracy

The Power Inquiry recommended a variety of reforms to the political system in the UK. However, we wish to focus on the work of two political scientists who present arguments for radical democratic change of particular relevance to critical community practice. Cohen and Fung argue for a substantial widening of democratic participation, along with a 'deliberative' approach to decision making that rests on processes of public reasoning rather than the process of interest aggregation, bargaining and exercises in 'power over' so characteristic of contemporary democracy. They see participative and deliberative democratic reform as the most effective corrective to what they call the 'democratic deficits of competitive representation' (Cohen and Fung, 2004).

'Competitive representation' is Cohen and Fung's term for 'actually existing democracy' – that is, democratic systems in which citizens exercise their political right to vote for representatives (generally of organised political parties), during periodic elections, thereby vesting in the winning candidates the authority *to shape public policy and exercise control* over the administration on their behalf.

Cohen and Fung outline the profound weaknesses of this form of democracy, drawing on the work of writers in the radical democratic tradition from Rousseau to Habermas, and they explain how 'radical democracy' significantly ameliorates such weaknesses. First, they suggest that increased levels of citizen participation and deliberation in decision making enhance *political equality*; the power of concentrated resources to influence the democratic process is reduced through an emphasis on 'the force of better arguments'. Enhanced participation, they argue, shifts 'the basis of political contestation from organised money to organised people' (Cohen and Fung, 2006, p 25).

Second, they suggest that radical democracy encourages greater levels of political responsibility. Their contention is that competitive representation is weak as far as ensuring official accountability is concerned; under competitive representation ordinary people are tempted to leave the hard work of policy making to professional politicians – and, as a consequence, the democratic skills, capacities and habits of the citizenry are apt to atrophy.

Finally, they argue that radical democracy fosters *political autonomy*, enabling citizens to live under rules that they have played a part in crafting for themselves:

in a deliberative democracy laws and policies result from processes in which citizens defend solutions to common problems on the basis of what are generally acknowledged as relevant reasons ... that express such widely shared democratic values as fairness, liberty, equal opportunity, public safety and the common good. (Cohen and Fung, 2004, p 26)

There are clear parallels between Cohen and Fung's analysis of the anticipated outcomes of radical democracy and our own attempts in Chapter Three to summarise the actual outcomes of 'participatory community governance' as illustrated in the case examples.

Cohen and Fung defend the theory of participatory and deliberative democracy from the charges of their detractors; that deliberative democrats are guilty of utopianism in believing that self and group interests can be trumped by the force of reasoning and better arguments. They concede that they do not expect self and group interests to disappear. However, as radical democrats they argue the aim is to:

ensure that political argument and appeals to interests are framed by considerations such as fairness, equality and common advantage. When citizens take these political values seriously, political decisions are not simply a product of power and interest: even citizens whose views do not win can see that the decisions are supported by good reasons. As a result, members can – despite disagreement – all regard their conduct as guided, in general terms, by their own reasons. (Cohen and Fung, 2004, pp 26–7)

Further, participatory democrats do not imagine that public governance will be amenable to direct participation by every citizen affected by every issue. In our Chicago case example, although the figure of 4,000 parents serving on the Local Schools Council at any given moment is an impressive number, it must be remembered that it is still a relatively small proportion of parents with school-age children. Universal deliberation on all issues of concern to all citizens is clearly an unrealistic goal; the point is that opportunities exist at all levels, and that obstructions to involvement are minimised.

Finally, and consistent with the previous point, Cohen and Fung point out that while seeking to maximise the full potential of participatory and deliberative democracy it has to be acknowledged that modern mass democracy must be organised, at least in part, on a system of competitive representation. Having said that, it also remains true that a fuller realisation of democratic values cannot be attained through competitive representation alone.

Critical theory: concluding comments

This discussion of radical democracy as an example of critical theory has only scratched the surface of a long and rich tradition in political thought, but it is impossible to go into further detail here. Our argument is that it *is* possible to develop a model of practice that includes an understanding of theory that

- helps practitioners to see the way that things can be different from what they are;
- offers an understanding of what needs to change;
- suggests a strategy for change that will be 'empowering' while also addressing the problems of disadvantage, exclusion and oppression in the communities with which they work.

The next section turns to an examination of critical action and an attempt to tease out – through a consideration of some of the difficulties and contradictions that commentators have highlighted when efforts are made to put such theory into action – the sort of issues that critical community practitioners must work to resolve if the potential of participatory community governance is to be realised.

Critical action

At the beginning of this chapter we made the point that effective critical community practice requires a step-change in opportunities available to 'active citizens' and 'active communities' to shape and implement policies and programmes that significantly frame the conditions of their lives. We noted that this often requires concerted action by policy makers and legislators, organisational managers and administrators, community workers and community educators, researchers and opinion formers.

In examining the third, 'critical action', component of the model, two analytical frameworks are introduced, in order to develop our argument. These are as presented in Figure 4.2 and Table 4.1. Once again, 'participatory community governance', as informed by the 'radical democracy project', is used as a practical example of critical community practice, to illustrate the arguments.

The scope of critical action

Figure 4.2 represents, in simplified form, the main 'sites' of critical community practice. Moving from left to right on the diagram, critical action entails working to generate a step-change in the paradigm (frame of reference), politics, policy, management and processes of community practice. This will necessarily entail a shift in the roles and activities of those occupations and activists with a 'community engagement' role: community workers and community educators, those involved in the management of community-led organisations (along with those responsible for introducing the institutional frameworks through which community organisations operate), as well as the politicians who pass the laws and 'will' the resources that make such a shift in practice possible. All of these actors, along with researchers, academics, think-tank personnel, media commentators and others, will be involved in progressing the debates and refining the thinking on which such underlying shifts in practice can be progressed. Most importantly, as the arrows in Figure 4.2 indicate, active citizens both as individuals and as members of communities have a central role in shaping such changes. Critical community practice rests on citizens and communities taking a key role in all of the sites identified: policy-making processes, programme leadership and management, participatory politics and so forth.

In Table 4.1 this framework is used to create a 6 × 6 table to further elaborate the dimensions and challenges of critical action.

- Along the top are arrayed the sites of critical action as identified in the previous figure, along with illustrative examples of the *kinds* of action pursued within each of them. Down the left-hand side

Figure 4.2: Critical community practice – sites

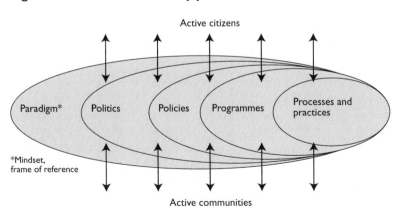

Table 4.1: Critical community practice – roles and tasks

	Paradigm change – shifts in public culture	Politics – legislative reform of governance policy; willing public resources to implement change	Policy development – institutional design of systems and structures for devolved community governance	Management of executive agencies – organisational building and leadership of managing agencies	Management of citizen agencies – organisation and management of organisations founded on participatory/deliberative democracy	Processes and practices – professional facilitation of enabling conditions
Public opinion shapers						
Politicians						
Policy makers						
Programme managers						
Professionals						
Active citizens and communities						

are the role players involved in such actions. This table is useful in drawing attention to the fact that in our model of critical action *all* these role players have a part to play in pursuing the actions to be taken in *all* sites. For example, in efforts to implement systems of participative and deliberative democracy, active citizens and communities, professionals and others all have an extended role to play in the tasks of politics and policy making – politics and policy are not, in other words, the exclusive preserve of politicians and their policy advisers. An examination of each *row* of cells suggests what each role player will need to consider in order to best engage in critical community practice.

• The table helps identify the range of competencies required for each task, as well as the particular action dilemmas likely to arise, and which need to be resolved if participative community governance is to be successfully realised. This issue is picked up in the next section.

Critical action: some key tasks and issues

Working for a paradigm shift in public culture entails building practical commitment to an imagined future. The critical community practitioner's task (be they policy planner, politician, professional workers in the community engagement field, or community organisations and active citizens) is to contribute to fashioning a convincing and concrete vision and agenda for change, in a way that makes real 'how things could be other than they currently are'. This is best achieved through an incremental 'action-learning' process, which involves addressing change issues across a broad range of policy and practice. We saw in our Brazilian case example in Chapter Three how involvement in participative and deliberative decision making on the annual city budget began to bring about a cultural shift in how city expenditure priorities were addressed in Port Alegre, and led to a very substantial increase in community involvement in the process. Practical action-learning can be augmented by other methods designed to tap citizen preferences and scope 'imagined futures', for example, a combination of such techniques as Planning for Real, Community Visioning, and Participatory Theatre (Smith, 2005, pp 31–2).

Our examples also showed how working for governance reform involves politicians determining and approving (through legislative action) the constitutional scope and remit of public accountability systems and budgets of devolved participatory decision making. Smith's review of 'co-governance' reforms (partnership boards, citizens' assemblies, community councils and so on) indicates that practical consideration needs to be given to 'incentives' for participation (most importantly that they *do* bring about change) to determine how participants in participatory fora are to be selected, and the extent and depth of power wielded through such decision-making processes (for example how broadly a forum's remit is cast; the extent of its capacity for agenda setting and so on) (Smith, 2005, pp 57-89).

Such political reform entails policy development, including, crucially, the design of the new institutional architecture necessary to make community power a reality in such devolved systems. We saw how in Chicago the institutional design of the system of Local Schools Councils effectively involved parents, teachers and community representatives in leading their schools, but also how in some 10 per cent of cases the system failed the schools, and had to be modified. The practicability and realism of such schemes in their early years seemed to be crucial (Smith, 2005, p 65).

Such institutional design generally entails the establishment of one or more levels of publicly accountable bureaucracy, along with systems for their management and leadership:

- development and leadership of ('arm's-length') agencies designed to approve, regulate and monitor the work;
- citizen-led organisations, which take the responsibility for leading, managing and delivering services, programmes and projects; and the
- establishment of partnership agencies capable of whole-system working, entailing co-leadership, joint management and inter-disciplinary team working.

As we saw in Chapter Three, none of the case example organisations examined there operated as totally free-standing bodies, unaccountable to other tiers of government. For example, in England, tenant-run housing associations operate under rules laid down by the Housing Corporation, a government agency set up to fund new and affordable social housing. This body operates a tenant empowerment programme designed to help tenants to challenge, influence or control how housing services are delivered in their communities. Such managing agencies have important roles to play in promoting and supporting effective and accountable participation and deliberation.

Organisational management of citizen-led agencies themselves is important in supporting those who participate: 'This can take various forms: training and mentoring; ensuring that the work demanded of active citizens is not unnecessarily burdensome or demanding and providing material support, rewards and compensation' (Rogers, 2004, p 34). This is partly about creating a culture and devising structures that, for example, reject overly long and excessively formal 'committee' type involvement. An Institute for Public Policy Research study argues the case for the imaginative use of innovative procedures to help make civic involvement 'engaging, even fun', rather than 'intimidating, exclusionary and boring'. It is also about providing child-care, out-of-pocket expenses and action-learning opportunities (Rogers, 2004, p 34). Effective organisational management often lies at the heart of the 'action' component of critical community practice. When active citizens become partners in running local schools and housing cooperatives, or become responsible for local renewal programmes, community enterprises or community health projects they inevitably assume leadership and management roles.

Finally, community workers, and other professional workers involved in community engagement and outreach activities for their agency or programmes have key roles to play in encouraging development of individual and organisational capacity for confident and effective involvement in participatory community governance. Informal community education, supporting community group and campaign work, building the capacity of local infrastructure (for example, meeting places, resource centres, community chest funding), along with agency outreach (health, educational, environmental and so on) all assist in further developing the stock of local 'social capital' that works as a powerful stimulus to engagement in wider processes of community governance.

Critical action: concluding comments

This discussion of the 'action' component of the model has underlined how critical action involves concerted action on a range of fronts by a diversity of actors. The conventional 'top-down, bottom-up' distinction so often invoked in discussions on community empowerment is transcended. Critical action entails *both* bottom-up *and* top-down action. It nearly always requires coordinated action by politicians and policy makers, organisational managers and 'community' professionals, as well as grass-roots community organisations and groups – a whole-systems approach – all of which involves, above all, deployment of a 'power with' approach.

These features of critical action pose particular challenges when we come to a consideration of 'critical reflection', the fourth component of our model, to which we now turn.

Critical reflection

It is now taken for granted that reflection 'in' and 'on' practice, as well as a preparedness to adopt a reflexive stance towards their work, has a vital part to play both in individual development *and* in organisational development. The implications of these commitments to critical practice are explored in this section.

Reflection: cognitive and emotional dimensions

In *How we think* (1986, originally published 1910) John Dewey aligned critical thinking with 'reflective thought' – 'to suspend judgment, maintain a healthy scepticism, and exercise an open mind' (Dewey, 1986, p 72). These three activities call for the active, persistent and careful consideration of any belief in light of the ground that supports it. Dewey suggests that reflective thought has both an intellectual and an *emotional* component. It entails the intellectual and emotional strength to go beyond the known without 'falling to pieces'. In this mode of analysis community practitioners poke, question, and reflect on what they have learned from their experience. Scepticism, questioning and open evaluation are essential – examine the problem, find and implement a solution, think about why you were or were not successful, and learn from your successes and failures. The process of reflection specifically involves 'standing back' from, and systematically reviewing, in a rigorous and patient way, what has been happening. In summary, reflective thinking involves the practitioner in *doing things* (probing, questioning, and so on) and *thinking about the things* they are doing (reflecting, evaluating feedback, and so on).

Reflexivity adds an additional dimension to reflection; it entails an ability to examine and reflect upon one's own thought and thought processes, to contextualise them (become critically aware of the context under which they have been shaped and under which they are deployed), and develop a capacity to modify them as a result of such inspection.

At the level of the individual worker, reflection is seen by Maureen Eby in a text on *Critical practice in health and social care* (Brechin et al, 2000), as the bedrock of practitioner development, and she goes on to quote with approval a definition offered by Quinn, that reflection is the ability to think and consider 'experiences, perceptions, ideas (values and beliefs) with a view to the discovery of new relations or the drawing of conclusions for the guidance of future action' (Quinn, 1998, p 122). A study of community practice (Butcher and Robertson, 2003) drew on the work of Boud et al (1985) in order to better understand 'reflection' in the context of individual learning, and the activities of the 'learning organisation' – and argued that embedding reflective processes was no less integral to effective development at the organisational level.

Adapting Boud's model to incorporate *critical* reflection involves the practitioner in the following processes:

- Mentally 'reliving' a particular experience; 'turning it over in our minds' as accurately and fully as possible.
- Paying attention to that experience in the light of what, above, we called 'critical consciousness'. This includes attending to feelings and reactions, and the emotions that the experience invokes. These may be 'positive' (helpful) or 'negative' (obstructive) emotions. In other words, emotional intelligence is exercised to deepen understanding of resultant feelings and where they 'come from'. Burying or denying feelings can prevent effective learning from experience. At the same time that component of critical consciousness is brought to bear that stresses reasoning, and evidence-based and creative thought. The experience is 're-viewed' from different perspectives, the critical practitioner appraises what has happened and then draws on critical theory to reach informed conclusions about the dynamics of what was happening. At the same time the capacity to evaluate experiences is enhanced by explicitly examining them through the lens of the guiding values and working assumptions that comprise the foundations of critical community practice.
- Reflecting on experience in the light of insights gained from a determined and rigorous use of the above processes leads to enhanced learning, which then becomes incorporated in the meaning structures that comprise the practitioner's critical consciousness.
- Finally, the learning that takes place is used to inform the future action of the critical practitioner. Regular reflection of this kind sets up a virtuous circle of action-reflection-learning-'more effective' action, and so on.

Organisational reflection

We emphasised above that critical action for participatory community governance involves a multiplicity of actors working at a variety of organisational levels. This raises an important question: how can the model of reflection outlined above be used *collectively*, accomplishing what might be called 'intra-' and 'inter-organisational' reflection? The idea of the 'learning organisation' can be of assistance here, as what we are considering in community contexts are 'network' forms of organisation. Paraphrasing Senge's (1990) key 'disciplines' of the learning organisation provides a basis for understanding organisational reflection: the following would seem to be crucial to ensuring collective reflection in multi-disciplinary network structures:

- *Systems thinking*: the discipline of reflecting on (as well as analysing and developing) network dynamics in holistic, systemic terms. This entails giving primacy to a consideration of interrelationships between network units, and only secondarily exploring the implications of what is happening to the dynamics for constituent organisations themselves.
- *Building shared vision*: Powerful generative learning from joint reflection will be most productive in its outcomes when people and organisations have developed a shared commitment to realising a shared future. This takes time and commitment to develop.
- *Team reflection*: Teams can be synergistic, they can encourage collaboration and energy flows that spark off thoughts and ideas such that outcomes are more than the sum of the parts. Authentic team-working in such network structures becomes a priority development.
- *Shared mental models and 'working assumptions'*: the powerful influence of 'taken for granted' ways of seeing things has already been emphasised. It is important that collective reflection works in such a way that organisational participants recognise the differences in the assumptions and models they use, and that they are willing to 'surface' them, and expose them to critical examination in a non-defensive manner.

Deliberative techniques – open-space events, ideas laboratories, consensus conferencing – (Gastil and Levine, 2005) deployed in semi-structured but highly participatory forums on a regular basis would seem to offer a promising way of engaging the actors involved in participatory community governance – from politicians to citizens – and in reflecting on their developing practice together.

Critical reflection: concluding comments

As already noted, it is now widely accepted that community work entails a commitment to reflection 'in' and 'on' practice. For the critical community practitioner such a commitment is even more important. Critical community practice involves moving outside the 'comfort zone' of one's peers; querying their conventional working assumptions and agreed value commitments, going beyond their standard theoretical understandings, and working in ways that transgress their accepted forms of action and intervention. Under such circumstances especially rigorous critical reflection on perspectives and practices is called for, to safeguard community interests, to underpin innovation, and to inspire the strength and confidence to 'go beyond the known without falling to pieces'.

Conclusions

At the beginning of this chapter it was pointed out that although discussing the component parts of the model separately has certain expository advantages, a possible down-side is a failure to see how the model works in an integrated, holistic way. This is overcome by envisaging the model in 'learning cycle' terms. In his classic theory of the 'experiential learning cycle', Kolb (1984) characterised much practice as a process of 'action-learning', as a continually turning cycle of action-reflection-conceptualisation-experimentation. Every piece of action may prompt the practitioner to reflect on what took place, and in an effort to make sense of this (and perhaps improve things next time round), such reflection can also lead to a review of the assumptions, values and theory used in order to interpret and deepen their understanding of the dynamics of their practice. This, in turn, can lead to what Kolb calls 'active experimentation' – a conscious attempt, 'the next time round', to do things differently, and to observe and reflect on *that* experience. Thus the practitioners' practice, as well as their mental map of 'how things are', develops and changes over time. Adopting this idea of experiential learning as a cyclical process helps both individuals (Kolb, 1984; Beard and Wilson, 2002) and organisations (Dixon, 1994; Nevis et al, 1995) to see how the insights of experiential learning can be deployed in a model of community practice (Butcher and Robertson, 2003). Envisaging the model presented in this chapter in experiential learning cycle terms means that it can be properly seen in both holistic terms (with the four key components working together), as well as in dynamic terms (with the processes described and analysed as elements in a continuing process of change).

FIVE

Working in and with community groups and organisations: processes and practices

Sarah Banks

Introduction

This is the first of three chapters exploring aspects of contemporary practice within the framework of the model presented in Chapter Four. Here the focus is on direct work in and with community groups and organisations. By 'direct work' we mean the face-to-face and organisational work accomplished by members in self-managed groups and by professional community workers and other professionals with a community focus in supporting, facilitating and advising community groups and organisations. Community groups and organisations may take many forms, ranging from loose networks to charities or businesses working for the benefit of geographical communities or communities of interest or identity. They may have a variety of functions, including campaigning, service delivery, policy making or self-help, for example.

The main focus of this chapter is on processes and practices of work in and with community groups and organisations. These processes and practices are embedded in a broader context of programmes, policies and paradigms (see Figure 4.2), which will be taken into account, although not explored in any depth in this chapter. The chapter discusses case studies of two community groups – a self-managed city-wide asylum seekers' network and a worker-supported neighbourhood residents' group. The work of the groups is analysed through first locating them in their political context, then exploring processes and practices for developing participants' critical consciousness – the core circle of Figure 4.1, which includes critical awareness of themselves in relation to the political context, commitment to the values of social justice and motivations and capacities for taking action.

Engaging active communities

As already discussed, community practice is about stimulating, engaging and achieving active communities. 'Active communities' include formal and informal organisations, groups and networks that exist in neighbourhoods or that are formed around common interests and identities. The use of the term 'active' emphasises the fact that these groups are involved in activities of mutual interest or for the collective good. If 'community' implies a sense of belonging, solidarity and significance among its members (which might be described as latent 'social capital'), the *active* community' is about mobilising this social capital. As noted in Chapter One, there is a growing emphasis in recent government policy in Britain and other countries on developing social capital and mobilising active communities, particularly in the context of neighbourhood and civil renewal (see, for example, Chanan, 2004; Home Office, 2004; Johansson and Hvinden, 2005; Newman, 2005; Social Exclusion Unit, 2001).

There are a number of reasons why policy makers, professional community practitioners and members of community groups themselves may seek to promote and develop active communities, which are summarised below.

1. *Active communities are regarded as good in themselves:* This may be based on an ideal concept of a democratic society, where each individual and group has a sense of belonging, a right to respect, to participate in decision making, to voice their opinions and so on.
2. *Active communities are regarded as means to desirable ends:* While active communities may be viewed as good for their own sakes, they also produce good outcomes. And this may be the main reason for promoting them. Examples of desirable ends include:
   - *Achieving specific desirable outcomes for their members, others, society or the planet:* Many people join community groups and organisations to work for specific goals for themselves or others. This may range from making friends and having the opportunity to meet with like-minded people to improving the local environment, saving a school or reducing atmospheric pollution. For example, a local Friends of the Earth group based in a small town holds coffee mornings, stalls in the local marketplace, meetings with expert speakers and works on specific campaigns on environmental issues at global, national and local level (for example, reducing global carbon emissions, promoting recycling nationally, cleaning up a

local river), with the aim of encouraging dialogue, education and creating a cleaner environment and fairer world.

- *Improving governance:* Current government policies in many countries are increasingly seeking to utilise the active community as a part of new structures of governance aimed at better policies and decision making. This involves giving a voice in planning and decision making and in the management of programmes and projects to people who are active in organisations in their neighbourhoods or communities of interest or identity. These people may be selected by, or simply regarded as representing or offering a voice from, specific communities or sectional interests. For example, local strategic partnerships set up as part of neighbourhood renewal policy in England to provide a strategic overview of needs in a district or borough are required to include representatives from the community sector to offer their perspectives. The example of local participatory budgeting in Port Alegre, Brazil described in Chapter Three had at its heart a more radical aim of achieving transformatory change in governance structures and relationships between citizens and the local state.

- *Revitalising civil society:* Creating active local communities is also seen as a way of mobilising social capital, creating a sense of belonging, reducing alienation and generating mechanisms for local social control. For example, the Friends Group of a city park has got a wide range of residents involved in restoring a bandstand which was formerly the haunt of drug users, organising hanging flower baskets for local houses and generally creating a sense of 'community spirit' and pride in the locality around the park.

- *Improving service delivery:* If representatives of local communities or communities of interest are involved in planning or delivering services this may improve their responsiveness and effectiveness. For example, young people play a key role in the management committee of a young people's centre – designing facilities and leading some of the groups and projects.

Given this range of very different ends, it is important that community practitioners have a critical awareness of their own reasons for doing the work, and how these may differ from those of employers, funders and diverse community participants. Recent British government programmes for neighbourhood and civil renewal, for example, place great emphasis on community participation. These requirements are encouraging the 'manufacture' of some community groups (for example, community partnerships) specifically for the purpose of contributing to local governance, with the result that these groups are burdened with bureaucratic requirements emanating from central government (Hodgson, 2004). Members of community groups themselves will have different motives for joining, and may find themselves in conflict with each other over priorities for action.

Nevertheless, arguably scope exists for some degree of critical community practice in all the areas of work mentioned above, but the extent to which it can be achieved will depend upon the features of context (locality, organisational constraints) and the levels of critical consciousness of the people involved (including their value commitments and capacity to take collective action). With this in mind, we have elaborated these key factors in the form of a series of questions, which will provide a framework for our discussion of two case examples, and may also be useful for practitioners to bear in mind when assessing, analysing, reviewing and evaluating the aims and purposes of the community groups of which they are a part.

- *Context:* How can *critical theorising* help us to understand the current state of affairs relevant to the community group or organisation in question? What structures and processes are contributing to disadvantage, exclusion and oppression? What is the history of community activity in this neighbourhood, identity or interest group? What sub-groups, interest groups, conflicts, discrimination or other barriers to collective action exist? How is power distributed and used? How does this relate to the distinction between 'power over' and 'power with' elaborated in Chapter Two? Whose agenda is paramount?
- *Critical consciousness: developing reflexive self-awareness, commitment and capacity:* How aware are the community practitioners and other participants of the contextual factors mentioned above, of the causes of social problems, of their own motivations and commitments, and their own role in perpetuating oppression and discrimination (reflexivity)? Are participants committed to the core values of critical community practice and motivated to work for change? Do they have the ability to engage in *critical reflection*, to deliberate, plan strategically, communicate, play an educative and supportive role and act as role models? Do they have the capacity to engage in *critical action* for social change? Do they have perseverance and determination to turn ideals into action?

Background to the case studies

We now explore two case studies of community-based work, using these as a way of focusing on the key dimensions of critical community practice. Both examples are based on information from individual and group interviews with community practitioners and relate to real organisations.[1] However, certain features of the people and organisations have been changed in order to preserve anonymity. The first case is based on the work of a city-wide asylum seekers' network – a self-managed group, with a very specific core purpose, formulated by the members of the group themselves, to defend asylum seekers' rights and oppose deportation. The second case focuses on a residents' group, set up by professional workers as part of an estate regeneration programme, with a number of purposes, not all of which are clear to, or owned by, its members.

Case study 1: The city-wide asylum seekers' network (ASN)

The asylum seekers' network (ASN) is a community action group consisting entirely of people who are involved on a voluntary basis. The information presented here is based on interviews with three British activists and a focus group of five asylum seekers of African origin who are members of a local committee of the network.

ASN was set up seven months ago in a large British city as 'a network or coalition aiming to unite people on the issue of political organisation to defend asylum seekers' rights and oppose deportation'. The group was formed following a regional meeting in a nearby town organised by a local representative of a national network of anti-deportation groups. This meeting was attended by a local representative of a national communist organisation, Joanne, who told the meeting that her group could offer support for people wanting to organise politically against deportation. This brought together an asylum seeker, a member of a socialist party working in an individual capacity, and a worker from a local voluntary organisation that supports asylum seekers. This core of people then organised two further public meetings in the city, culminating in the formation of ASN, structured as a loose network of groups and individuals, comprising asylum seekers, refugees (asylum seekers who have been granted asylum) and British activists.

Membership is not formalised, and the level of members' activities varies from several times a week to once every few months. Some members take action through means such as sending faxes to try and prevent imminent deportations, but rarely see other members of the network face to face. At present, the weekly meetings typically involve between 5 and 20 people, the majority normally asylum seekers, while demonstrations have involved between 40 and 70 people. ASN is linked informally with the national network of anti-deportation groups, and, through its organisational members, to a national communist organisation and a regional network for the integration of migrants from a particular African country.

The main local activities have included: regular local information and planning meetings; pickets of the local Immigration Service Reporting Centre twice a month; a demonstration in the centre of the city calling for the right to work for asylum seekers; a 'Big Noise' demonstration with pots and pans outside the local reporting centre; participation in the regional May Day rally for International Workers' Day – when an asylum seeker from the group spoke from the platform; educational meetings explaining asylum seekers' legal and housing rights; campaigns against individual deportations; establishing more locally based groups in specific parts of the city; the initiation of a national day of action outside Immigration Service Reporting Centres; a march through the centre of the city and demonstration outside the local offices of the National Asylum Support Service; and participation in demonstrations elsewhere in Britain.

As a relatively new group, ASN is constantly evolving in terms of its membership, structure and aims. It has also experienced some conflict over the role of the political organisations in the group, and the direction of the group in general. As Joanne, the initiator of the group, commented: 'The people that don't like communists accuse our group of dominating.' Yet it was acknowledged by several members of the committee that, hitherto, the success of the group's activities has relied heavily on the knowledge, commitment and motivation of the British political activists who have experience in their own political organisations. The long-term aim, however, is to build the confidence and knowledge of the asylum-seeker members of the network, so that they can take on more of the responsibility themselves.

Discussions with committee members indicated some areas of disagreement and debate over the balance of the work of the group between campaigning work (including demonstrations) and support for individuals (legal and moral support, as well as material support in terms of finance, childcare and accommodation). Joanne described her motivation for starting the group as being linked to her voluntary work for a church-led charity that was trying to help asylum seekers:

Every week you'd be faced with people that were really depressed and sometimes suicidal, telling me all sorts of awful stories ... And it seemed to me that you needed to organise something with asylum seekers, and that the situation for asylum seekers was only going to get worse. Because if you look at what the problems are, then why were people destitute, with only five pounds a week from a charity? It was because their asylum case had been failed, so it was the asylum system that was unfair, because when you talked to those people, and their stories, it was confusing as to why they'd been failed, when they came from countries like the Congo, where there was a war ... I think one of the factors is just the worsening situation for asylum seekers in this country, and that's led to the conditions where people ... supportive of asylum seekers want to do something, to organise politically.

The two other British activists interviewed echoed this point, one of whom, Colin, worked as a mental health social worker and came across asylum seekers through his job, while the other had worked for a charity working for asylum seekers. Both felt that there was a need for a group that would campaign for asylum seekers. For the asylum seekers themselves, the fact that ASN was an independent group was stressed as important, as François commented:

What motivated me to join was that it was an organisation, which stood on behalf of asylum seekers, an independent organisation with no government backing.

Other asylum seekers echoed this view, seeing ASN as fighting for the interests of asylum seekers as a group and offering practical help to individuals in relation to detention, deportation and immigration.

Context: community action for social justice

The ASN developed out of concerns about the growing problems facing asylum seekers coming to Britain. Financial and housing assistance, opportunities to work and criteria for judging asylum cases have recently become tighter in Britain and other countries (Cohen et al, 2002; Griffiths et al, 2005; Hayes, 2005; Zetter et al, 2005). For example, in Britain, despite steadily falling numbers of applicants, in the second quarter of 2006, 80 per cent of initial asylum applications were refused, and 73 per cent of appeals were dismissed (Home Office, 2006). At the same time, workforce migration from Poland and other European Union accession states has been encouraged, alongside targeted initiatives to attract highly skilled workers to meet the needs of the economy (Chinweizu, 2006). In Britain, the cumulative effect of recent legislation has been simultaneously to deprive asylum seekers of various social rights, while creating a separate and inferior system of welfare support, involving low-level subsistence via money or vouchers, compulsory dispersal and no choice in housing allocation (Humphreys, 2004). A centralised agency, the National Asylum Support Service, coordinates arrangements for asylum seekers in dispersal areas. The disadvantage faced by asylum seekers in terms of material resources is very stark, with asylum seekers receiving, at the most, 30 per cent less benefit than the minimum income support for British nationals in 2006.

Asylum seekers who have had their applications refused frequently have all welfare support cut off, and continue to be denied the right to work legally. This situation often remains for long periods even where asylum seekers have entered a fresh claim. This exacerbates the social exclusion of asylum seekers, who are isolated from their home countries, without citizenship rights and largely without possibilities to participate in employment, voting or other civic action (serving on boards, committees, juries and so on). Furthermore, they are frequently subject to discrimination and oppression, stemming from negative public perceptions and stereotyping of asylum seekers as a burden on the host country, and harsh and often racist treatment by the authorities and some neighbours.

ASN is an organic group, formed and run by community activists, with the aim of working for social change through empowering asylum seekers to participate in political debates; educating politicians, policy makers and the public about the injustices of the asylum system; organising to bring pressure for legislative changes; and fighting individual cases. Although ASN targets local offices and fights local cases, it is also part of the national networks and organisations; it operates mainly through campaigning, and the issues on which it works can be viewed as part of both national government policy and global problems associated with inequality and exploitation between rich and poor countries, and the wars, nationalism and racism which follow.

The three British activists who were interviewed all had voluntary or paid work experience where they had seen the effects on individual asylum seekers and had been involved in offering help. But they felt there was a need to go further, to challenge the root causes of the problems, which lay in increasingly punitive government policies and negative and often racist attitudes among some sections of the British public, fuelled by hostile media coverage and the presentation by the government of immigration as the source of a multitude of problems. Asylum seekers often have language difficulties and are unaware of their rights, the workings of the British legal and political system or potential sources of information and support. They may feel rejected, powerless and dehumanised. One of the valued achievements of ASN identified by an asylum seeker member, Grace, was:

> to get involved in so many things that would make people feel like a human being ... Because as an asylum seeker, the people don't classify us as a human being, so they make us to feel as humans sometimes. So I think that is some of the achievement.

The involvement of political activists from communist, socialist and anarchist organisations in such campaigning groups is not uncommon, but it can cause some tensions between different political trends, as well as between the committed and experienced political activists and other less politically motivated group members. In this group there had been some disagreements about a number of issues, including: what tactics to use (some members wanting to 'de-radicalise' the campaign in order to gain trade union backing and some asylum seekers fearing their cases might be jeopardised by participating in national demonstrations); about how much the group could or should be involved in giving individuals material help as opposed to focusing on campaigning (the latter meaning it cannot be a registered charity); and about whether to allow broader political literature on the ASN stall.

Some of the issues about tactics can be linked to the distinction developed in Chapter Two between 'power over' and 'power with'. The political activists in the group were certainly keen to work alongside asylum seekers and refugees in running the group. As one of the British activists, Colin, said: 'It's acted as a campaigning group, but a campaigning group not for asylum seekers, but of asylum seekers.' So in terms of internal organisation, the approach adopted in deciding on aims, tactics, ways of organising and developing the group was one of 'power with'. However, the main external tactics (campaigning, protest marches and demonstrations) adopted the approach of 'power over' – seeing the relationship of ASN with the Home Office, National Asylum Support Service and Reporting Centres as a conflictual one. Given the relative powerlessness of the asylum seekers, and the dense and impenetrable national systems put in place to support and control them, campaigning, noisy protests and legal challenges are obvious tactics to use. These are also a traditional part of the repertoire of the political groups involved in ASN.

Similar tensions and issues can be found in many other campaigning groups that focus on challenging repressive policies or practices, where individuals directly affected are working alongside supporters and members of political groupings concerned about the broader issues of social justice. Another classic example in Britain was the anti-poll tax campaign (Banks and Noonan, 1990).

Developing critical consciousness: awareness, commitment and capacity

Consciousness-raising is a key part of the ASN's aims. First, the British activists and those asylum seekers and refugees more experienced in campaigning and networking are keen to help other asylum seekers to see that their problems lie not just in incompetence or ill-will on the part of local officials, but in a large-scale system of unjust policies and practices. Second, they need to fight not just individual cases or local services, but attitudes of the public as a whole, politicians, policy makers and social welfare professionals. These may be driven by deep underlying causes, such as the labour needs of the British economy, and the availability of labour from other sources such as EU accession countries, making them even more difficult and complex to change. Third, the campaigning, protests, leaflets and media coverage are one way of starting a process of deliberative civic action by making the public and others aware of the asylum seekers' perspectives and the plight that they face. This is about challenging the discourse of 'scrounging' and arousing the public conscience, as well as developing the confidence, skills and 'power within' of the asylum seekers in the group.

The ASN is clearly a group with the values of social justice at its very heart, stressing those aspects that are about solidarity and working together for transformational change. The British political activists see the work of ASN as part of a broader struggle on behalf of oppressed people. As Joanne commented: 'ASN wasn't set up to be a charity, it was solidarity not sympathy.' This has evolved into a recent focus on opposition to the National Asylum Support Service system. This approach is based on the argument, as summarised by one of the other British communist group members, that the existence of a parallel and separate welfare system for asylum seekers not only allows for the inferior treatment of asylum seekers, but actively divides them from working-class British people:

> They may face similar problems such as poor housing, unemployment and lack of access to transport and other services, but because they experience this via different representatives of the state, they are encouraged to view their interests and problems as separate to and even antagonistic to those of asylum seekers. Communist members of ASN have put forward this analysis in working-class areas where ASN has local committees, in an attempt to involve working-class people on the basis of solidarity rather than sympathy, by linking the problems of asylum seekers to British people's own problems, and avoiding a competition of who is the worst off.

Part of the purpose of the group is also to bring together isolated asylum seekers and develop a sense of solidarity among them. Yet at the same time the group is very heterogeneous, with members having different understandings of the nature and causes of the problems, and varying in their capacity and confidence to take action. Joanne has a clear Marxist political analysis, regarding asylum seekers as part of the working class, 'subject to oppression by an imperialist state', seeing her work with asylum seekers as part of a global political movement. Some of the other members of the group do not share, or even understand, this analysis. For many of the asylum seeker members and some British members, their concern is essentially reformist – to be able to impress upon the British authorities the ways in which the system is not working for them, and seeking improvements in childcare, education, housing and the legal processes. Furthermore, for many there is a very real fear that by participating in demonstrations they might jeopardise their individual cases for asylum in the UK. This is intensified by many asylum seekers' experiences of the very different political role of the police between their countries of origin and that currently existing in Britain, giving them exaggerated expectations of the response of the state to peaceful protests. François suggested that some people were tending to withdraw from the group because it was too political:

> People have a fear of demonstrations due to the fact – it depends on your standpoint, your asylum claim where it is. As [solicitor] said, that you have to be careful if you know that you're a person who's standing maybe on a thin

line, you really have to be careful. So people are scared of
participating in the demonstrations. Fear.

Grace's recommendation for the group was to: 'focus on asylum
issues and forget about politics'. This view was taken even further by
another asylum seeker who suggested that the visibility of a communist
organisation in ASN's activities was unhelpful:

> When we do the things, the communist organisation will
> be there, and its slogan will be there, so we are caught in
> between. Which means that if those slogans are not put
> – if we are demonstrating and the communist organisation
> doesn't go in within ASN, then I think it will be more
> fine.

At the same time, asylum seekers have also been involved in ASN who
themselves have substantial political experience, gained both in their
country of origin and in Britain, and an analysis which sees a need
for wider political action. Therefore, the conflicts over reformism and
the very purpose of ASN have cut across the divide between asylum
seekers and British activists. It would be misleading to view the situation
simply in terms of reformist asylum seekers and radical British activists.
These struggles are fluid, and the positions that even specific individuals
have occupied within them have changed over time. How the group
tackles these issues is in the process of emerging. It is too easy to suggest
that the caution expressed by some of the asylum seekers is based on
internalised oppression and a lack of critical consciousness about the
causes of their plight. The debate seems to be more about ownership of
the group and its tactics. The comments quoted above were expressed
in a focus group of asylum seekers conducted as part of the research
for this chapter. The focus group provided a safe opportunity, outside
a business meeting, for participants to explore, test and develop ideas
about principles, aims and tactics. Because of the focus group's purpose
(to hear all and any ideas) and its format (explicitly dialogical rather
than argumentative), it had some of the qualities outlined by Habermas
(1990) as an ideal speech situation. For community action groups
such as this, which are at an early stage of development and where
membership is very diverse, the opportunity for critical dialogue with
each other about purposes and approaches is both useful and part of
a learning process.

These discussions within the group about its focus, activities and
public image reflect differences in reasons for involvement in the

group, individuals' own circumstances in relation to their asylum cases, political ideologies and paradigms and views about tactics. Nevertheless, all members were committed to working to improve circumstances for asylum seekers and the skills and strengths of the political activists were greatly valued, as one asylum seeker commented:

> I think one of the strengths of ASN so far is, may I call it the motivating nature of some of the members, especially the founding members. Some of them are so persistent to issues, not minding the interest, or the participation of other members. Some people will just volunteer to go out of their way to achieve anything they want to achieve. For instance in doing demonstrations even while some people are not showing interest. Some people will volunteer to carry on the whole work.

As one of the British members of the group observed, at the early meetings, the common factor uniting people who took part was:

> a sense of outrage at government policy in relation to asylum seekers, and a sense that what was happening was grossly immoral, that it was probably illegal, and that there was a need for something to be done about it.

This member expressed his values in terms of justice and fairness, believing that people have a right to claim asylum and to be treated decently when they come to Britain seeking asylum. The initial commitment of group members to work for individual and collective justice, often linked with emotions such as anger, seems to be developing and deepening through the process of working together.

Case study 2: The estate residents' community action partnership (CAP)

In our earlier book, *Managing community practice*, we included a case study from the manager of a seven-year regeneration programme (see Banks, 2003a). The programme covered a small housing estate (2,000 residents in public and housing association properties) on the edge of a city. One of the issues we discussed was the challenges this manager faced in trying to encourage local residents to participate meaningfully in the partnership board that managed the £13 million budget. The manager also described her reservations about the proposals that came from the residents to build a new community resource centre in the middle of the estate. She was concerned about the sustainability of such a centre in terms of whether there would be sufficient usage and whether the residents would be able to manage it on their own after the regeneration programme had ended.

The funding for the resource centre was obtained from a variety of sources and we take up the story again now when the building is finished and in use. This time the account is based on interviews with two community development workers, John and Joan, whose job it is to support the residents in managing the building; an interview with Jimmy, a resident now working as a volunteer support worker; and several visits to, and observations at, the community resource centre where the community action partnership is based.

A community action partnership was set up on the estate several years previously by regeneration workers. It grew out of an earlier community forum, whose purpose was to provide a focus for communication between local residents and the regeneration workers and partnership board, as well as to stimulate and take action on the estate. Following a successful bid for funding (supported by the Regeneration Partnership and other funding bodies) to build a new community resource centre on the estate, the CAP formed a management committee, which became the group to which the new initiative belonged. It was their role to contribute towards the design and furnishing of the centre, and to manage it when finished.

According to John, the senior community development worker, who was appointed the previous year as the centre was being built, the CAP management committee was in disarray. Its membership had recently changed completely after a round of elections, and those who were now involved had little idea of what managing a building entailed or what their role should be. Nor did they seem eager to learn, or to take any responsibility. Four of the six members of the committee were completely new and were elected as part of a 'coup d'état' by residents from one part of the estate. John commented:

> A resident is supposed to be my manager. But she is 72 and she's quite ill and she's had a stroke recently, plus she has no knowledge of the work ... She doesn't know how to manage me.
>
> This management committee destroys itself from within, because of internal politics and power struggles. And I think it very much comes down to they haven't been properly

trained in what they're supposed to be doing, and also …
they don't know how to make a point or raise an issue.

John described how he had booked all the new management committee
members on to a communications course, but none of them had
turned up:

> How do you empower people if you can't train them? We
> are very aware that we've got a short time-scale here, we've
> only got two years left. And we're trying to get this across
> to the residents without scaring them too much, because I
> think it is very scary.

Several months after her appointment, the other community
development worker, Joan, investigated the possibility of holding a 10-
week 'Learning about community work' course that was being offered
to community groups and organisations by a regional community work
learning partnership. Joan trained as a tutor and co-facilitated the course
in the centre, recruiting a mixture of 13 residents and regeneration/
community workers from the estate and elsewhere. Joan felt that the
success of the course in engaging the interest and motivation of local
people was due to the fact that it was held in the centre, it focused
on issues and skills of immediate relevance and she was a tutor. As she
commented: 'Because I was doing it, it was safe, because I'd built up
relationships with the people.' She was, however, under no illusions
that this course was just a starting point:

> It was working through some of the experiences they
> [residents] were having, whether negative or obstructive or
> whatever they may be, to look at the underlying reasons why
> that might be. So there was some first-level learning, but
> they never really got to move on to the political processes.
> It was still dealing with the regular daily community
> engagement part.

Jimmy was one of the nine people who completed the course, having
initially come into the centre as a volunteer and newcomer to the estate.
He felt it was a very positive experience, giving him confidence to apply
for the volunteer coordinator job in the centre, creating links with other
residents and professional workers and encouraging reflection about
what could be done to involve more people and improve the estate:

> It made us think a lot about going on to our estate, asking
> people what they wanted, and going to people and saying:
> 'Look, we want ... for our community'. Whereas before
> we all just sat and waited for it to come to us, and of course
> it doesn't.

Context: inter-agency neighbourhood regeneration

CAP needs to be understood in the context of persisting problems of
poverty and social exclusion and past and present government policies
towards neighbourhood regeneration and community participation
(Lupton, 2003; Mayo and Robertson, 2003). Current policies stress
multi-agency and partnership working, including involving local
representatives, as part of a strategy to solve intractable social and
economic problems (Balloch and Taylor, 2001; Gilchrist, 2003). Yet,
the very intensity of the gaze of all the agencies and their obsession
with reaching targets can be seen as part of a control and surveillance
role. The attempt to incorporate community groups, while offering
some scope for shared decision making, can at the same time result in
a co-option of these groups, with a resulting loss of 'critical edge' as
they too begin to work towards 'shared' targets and outcomes.

A critical analysis of the context reveals issues common to much
community work – the problem of how to mobilise local communities
and work with conflict and divisions (Ledwith, 2005; Popple, 1995;
Ronnby, 1995). In this particular case, an estate that has been in decline
for many years was chosen for a large-scale investment of funding, with
a requirement for resident participation. A flood of professional workers
from police, health, housing associations, education, services for children
and youth and various voluntary organisations set up projects in order
to reduce unemployment, crime, drug use, homelessness and so on. The
agendas were created from outside, and residents were expected not
only to play a part in decision making, but to take responsibility for
implementing some of the schemes. One of John's reflections was:

> The residents' view of regeneration is different from
> the regeneration team. The regeneration team exists on
> quantities, facts, figures and numbers ... Their [residents']
> idea is about quality of life and service provision.

While CAP is strictly speaking a 'self-managed group', it has received a
considerable amount of support from professional workers. The workers
initially involved in supporting and developing CAP were employed

as community workers as part of the time-limited regeneration programme. John is keen to develop the management committee so that it can take over the running of the centre when he leaves. But with no history of self-managed community groups on the estate and a legacy of conflict between two sides of the estate, the task seems almost overwhelming – or 'scary'.

In contrast to the asylum seekers' network, CAP could be described as being towards the 'manufactured' end of the spectrum of community groups, in that it was set up when the estate became designated as a regeneration area in order to play a role in the regeneration process. Although CAP had the potential to develop organically and to use its position to play a powerful role in the estate regeneration (even to challenge some of the large organisations on the partnership board), it had not done so. Unlike the asylum seekers' network, its aims are not inherently radical – indeed, its members do not seem to have a clear sense of purpose or strategy. This is where the workers have a role in helping local residents clarify purpose and develop tactics. Indeed, they could work with the residents to look back in time and look around themselves in the wider world and ask questions about why they have a community resource centre, why the estate has been subject to regeneration schemes, and why it is such a struggle to involve people in the running and use of the resource centre.

Recent research undertaken by Williams (2005) suggests that the drive to equip people in the most deprived neighbourhoods with the skills and competence to participate in formal community organisations may be inappropriate. He argues, using evidence from the General Household Survey, that the participatory culture of relatively deprived neighbourhoods and social groups tends towards one-to-one aid (such as helping neighbours), rather than joining local organisations. Williams suggests that greater recognition and value needs to be given to what he calls 'informal' community involvement (see also Burns et al, 2004, pp 127–8; Taylor, 2003). This would imply that community practitioners should focus more on supporting/developing organic as opposed to manufactured groups.

Developing critical consciousness: awareness, commitment and capacity

When the senior community development worker, John, was interviewed, in the year after the building was completed, the CAP group was unaware of the core purpose and values of community practice (let alone critical community practice) and did not seem motivated to work for change. John suggested that residents had been consulted many times and their views had been ignored:

> People know that when they're being consulted, the chances
> are that what they say will not make a jot of difference
> because the regeneration of the estate will happen in the way
> that it's down in the appraisals anyway. And as a result, I think
> it's been very difficult to develop an active community.

How can critical community practitioners (in this case, the two workers) begin the process of critical consciousness-raising in the kind of situation described above? As noted earlier, Paulo Freire (1972, 1993) talks about 'conscientisation' (developing critical political consciousness) as opposed to 'domestication' (acceptance of the status quo). We may recall that Freire, in his work with peasants in South America who could not read or write, developed an approach that incorporated literacy with political education, starting from people's everyday experiences in their localities (see also Hope et al, 1994; Kirkwood and Kirkwood, 1989; Ledwith, 2005). In the case described above, the question is how to offer some education that residents feel comfortable with, motivated to participate in, and that links with their role in their local community. The 'Learning about community work' course offered the chance for a group of residents (not just management committee members, some of whom had left by then) to learn some basic skills in community work, and to reflect on the nature of their own neighbourhood and its issues and problems. The course included discussion of the values of community development work, and examples of community groups taking action.

This is one starting point in helping to develop a consciousness of where power lies in a community, through a dialogical process, while at the same time learning some basic skills. Clearly Joan's critical analysis of the situation, including the current capacities of the residents and the pace at which they could learn, played a key part in beginning this work. Although she felt they had not really moved towards developing critical political consciousness, this course was a necessary first stage. According to Jimmy, one of the course participants, this seemed to have served as a stimulus to begin to develop more commitment and confidence (for critical discussion of the value of such courses, see Banks and Vickers, 2006).

While Joan acknowledged that, by the time the course was over, it was too late to begin to challenge the regeneration partnership (which was coming to an end), if community workers can do further work alongside the residents to build their confidence, then eventually some changes may occur. Joan spoke of 'mentoring' various residents and allowing them to shadow her as she worked. This was very time-consuming, but she felt it was a safe and constructive way to build skills, confidence and commitment. Joan was acting both as a role model and an informal educator (two key roles of the community development worker). The perseverance required is considerable, as is the time, which is why short-term programmes with community workers who move on quickly are not ideal for facilitating critical community practice in areas like this. The process of developing commitment to the critical community practice values and processes of social justice, emancipation and empowerment is at a very early stage for the CAP group, and will be an ongoing educational process.

Conclusions

We have analysed two different types of community group. The asylum seekers' network, with its campaigning focus, national and global links, and the involvement of highly active left-wing political organisations fits the paradigm of radical community action, but faces challenges due to the diversity of backgrounds and motivations of network members. Nevertheless, we noted how the commitment of all group members to work for change, often fuelled by anger at injustice, is developing and deepening through the process of taking collective action. Some of the features of this process can be identified as follows:

- *the experience of solidarity* between asylum seekers from different areas and also with British participants;
- *education and consciousness-raising* about asylum seekers' rights and unjust systems and practices;
- *role modelling* by experienced activists and the development of skills, confidence and courage through experiencing action;
- *deliberation* about aims, purposes and tactics as part of a constant process of revision and renegotiation.

The community action partnership is a more locally based and homogenous group, which, despite its name ('community action') has more of a focus on running a centre and service provision. The process of developing commitment and capacity for critical community action is only just beginning and is being initiated by paid community workers. The approaches have comprised much more explicitly educational processes, such as formal courses, including:

- *education* through learning about the potential for community work and working together in a structured course with other participants;
- *mentoring* by one of the community workers, who also acted as a role model.

We can identify some common features in the processes of the groups' development, particularly: the importance of education, consciousness-raising and mentoring/role modelling by experienced practitioners.

Our discussion of these two examples highlights the importance of, and the challenges in, developing opportunities for participants in community groups to learn from each other through dialogue and debate, to be aware of alternative perspectives, to locate their own problems and issues in a broader picture and to become politically aware in terms of both the analysis of their own situations and the tactics to use to bring about transformational change. This requires a process of learning, which can be unplanned and informal as part of group activities, whereby participants develop their levels of awareness and competence through experience and reflection on their experience. It can also be planned, yet informal (as in the case of experienced people mentoring the less experienced) or formal (through education and training programmes or structured supervision). In Chapter Eight we explore in more detail some of the ways of developing the critical community practitioner.

Note

[1] We are grateful to the members of the community groups who gave up their time to be interviewed and to contribute to the focus group. We are particularly grateful to Tom Vickers, who conducted the focus group and some of the interviews, and for his helpful comments on sections of this chapter.

SIX

Critical community practice: organisational leadership and management

Hugh Butcher and Jim Robertson

Introduction

Throughout this book we have stressed that community practice is not the preserve of any one professional or functional group in society. In this chapter our focus is on those practitioners who contribute to community practice through their role as organisational managers and leaders of community programmes and projects.

Such managers and leaders have been subject to ever increasing 'white-water change' (Vaill, 1996) over the recent past, buffeted by a host of policy imperatives and their associated targets and responsibilities. In this chapter we discuss the ways in which a range of – often contradictory – demands on those who are responsible for the organisation, management and leadership of community initiatives has proved both taxing and relentless. We argue that such continuous change has often pushed organisational leaders and managers into ad hoc and partial responses, the consequence being that they fail to develop organisational strategies capable of coping with the change imperatives in a measured and coherent way.

However, the challenge to organisational management and leadership has not been wholly attributable to the volume of change. Policy demands for community engagement and involvement in themselves offer significant challenges to taken-for-granted methods of managing and leading not-for-profit, community and public sector organisations. Much organisational management and leadership is still based on a corporate 'professional-bureaucratic' approach, and this prompts the question: how do models of organisational management and leadership need to evolve and change in order to become fit for purpose for contemporary community practice work undertaken with and through an empowered, active citizenry?

Additional challenges arise as a result of seeking to implement *critical* approaches to community practice of the kind illustrated in Chapter Three under the heading of 'participatory community governance'.

In this chapter these questions are approached using the four-fold lens of critical community practice outlined in Chapter Four. First, we begin with some *critical reflections* on the current state of organisational management and leadership of community practice in the context of continuous 'white-water change'. We then move on to present an argument (informed by critical theorising) for new approaches to organisational management and leadership that are consistent with the assumptions, values and dispositions embraced by critical consciousness. Thus, finally we are in a position to sketch out a 'fit-for-purpose' model of critical action for organisational management and leadership – revisiting, for illustrative purposes, some of the case examples of participatory community governance presented in Chapter Three.

The challenge of 'white-water' change

Community practice and the public sector

Public sector organisations are currently experiencing enormous changes, and further changes undoubtedly lie ahead. As outlined in Chapter One, in the UK there exists a complex range of government community policies focusing on a diverse range of problems, and community practice managers in all sectors are called upon to exercise leadership and take responsibility for programmes concerned with deprivation and poverty, anti-social behaviour and social exclusion, as well as programmes targeted at worklessness, local economic development, and community planning, to name but a few! Government social policies are increasingly predicated on an expanded role for third-sector social enterprise, on the basis of this sector's ability to encourage citizen involvement in project planning and delivery, and this places further responsibility on public sector managers to work in and through partnerships. This expansion will be given further impetus as government policy promotes the contracting out of services currently delivered by the public sector, and as a response to further EU funding streams (Hudson, 2003; HM Treasury, 2005).

Many managers are experiencing (as a local government officer said at a conference on local authority community development [Bishop et al, 2006]) a 'policy nightmare', where 'certainty of role and purpose are becoming increasingly blurred'. At the same time, pondering on the way government departments are pushing forward the community engagement agenda, the same senior manager said:'The time has never been better for community development'!

There is certainly evidence of a shift in focus, and it is one which has significant implications for practice management. From a community practice perspective this is only the latest in a number of shifts in focus. Municipal government has been party to a long series of changes over recent years. The current growth of community oriented policies involving the construction of community strategies in partnership with a variety of other stakeholders, including community sector groups, is a relatively new experience for many local authorities. But commentators remind us that as recently as the 1980s a wide range of legislation sought to specifically *dis*-empower local government from carrying out effective community governance roles. The sale of council housing, deregulation in public transport, marginalisation of Health Boards, the capping of expenditure, increasing centralisation through Urban Development Corporations and capital spending controls, and the switch in governance of further education and some higher education sectors all significantly reduced the ability of local government to provide effective community governance through its traditional role of delivering services. Reorganisation in these earlier times was about reducing the power of the local state (Banks et al, 2003; Butcher et al, 1993). It is not surprising, given the demands placed on them, that many local politicians and their officers find the challenge of yet further change confusing and raise questions about where their work and responsibilities are heading.

Research shows that public service organisations, understandably, become absorbed in the requirements of continuity; services have to be provided in response to increasing demand, often against the backcloth of reduced funding and resources; targets have to be met in response to the organisation's priorities and central government demands. In such an environment, factors and forces can work against the prospect of positive and productive change. It must also be noted that long-established organisations, like local authorities, have an institutional 'memory' that privileges certain ways of doing things and makes discussing and managing change difficult. Relationships have been built up over the years with powerful interest groups whose influence is pervasive and embodied in policies and ways of thinking. Thus, expectations of local authorities and other public organisations often find it difficult to free themselves from a history of past actions and embedded practices (Ranson and Stewart, 1994).

Community practice and the not-for-profit and community sectors

It is now recognised that community, social, cultural and, more recently, economic development all depend on a diverse and healthy not-for-profit sector. Community development is substantially based on non-profit organisations such as faith groups, community groups, community centres and action groups. Likewise, social development is based on local and national networks of organisations for health, disability, social welfare and campaigning groups for almost every facet of human and animal life. Non-profit organisations and community groups play a critically important role in the democratic process. They are also renowned as the instigators of new ideas and social innovations (Hudson, 2003).

Yet managers of these organisations have been far from exempt from the consequences of white-water change. They also face a new set of questions about how to further the contribution of their organisations and about how they should manage and direct their efforts. There are demands that non-profit organisations should report on the results they achieve, in addition to reporting on their activities and finances. There is pressure to form strategic alliances and partnerships with the public and private sectors and to achieve ever more demanding goals. There is increasing regulation, sometimes from bodies that have different and conflicting requirements. As Deakin (2001) and others indicate, these are just a few of the many challenges that managers (as well as practitioners) now face in the voluntary and community sectors, just as they are faced by their public sector colleagues.

Organisational responses to change: problems and weaknesses

The organisational management and leadership responses to such changes have often been seen as less than helpful. Figure 6.1 summarises some of the more common criticisms of such responses.

To spell out these reactions in a little more detail:

1. *A reactive, fire-fighting approach; short-termism:* The day-to-day experience of many managers and practitioners is often one of 'fire-fighting', managing demanding time constraints, setting difficult priorities, negotiating tricky relationships, finding short cuts, dealing with stress; and while feeling accountable and responsible, at the same time feeling powerless and lacking any real autonomy. A 'reactive'

Figure 6.1: Organisational management of community practice – challenges, problems and weaknesses

Public and not-for-profit organisational management of community practice is often characterised by:

1. A reactive, 'fire-fighting' approach and 'short-termism'.
2. Ad-hoc, project- and programme-based approaches to community practice – a 'top-down, target-driven, inspection heavy, quest for big solutions'.
3. An insular and inward-looking organisational stance; the 'silo' mentality.
4. A value placed on organisational continuity, based on institutional memory about 'how we do things around here', which is deeply embedded in patterns of relationships and organisational processes.
5. A focus on operational issues and contingencies.
6. A corporate 'professional-bureaucratic' model of organisations and service provision. Top-down development of policies and plans by policy makers/ politicians, implemented by bureau-professionals.
7. An overwhelming sense of 'bombardment' by the number, range and complexity of political and policy demands for community-based policy and programmes, 1997–2006 (the 'policy nightmare').

approach to problem solving is often the result (Fish and Coles, 1998).

Further, few local authorities have, until recently, sought to adopt coherent community strategies to inform their policies and procedures. This is not to undervalue the many excellent community projects that were initiated by some statutory organisations in partnership with some of the larger community development organisations in the voluntary sector. Unfortunately, however, many of these have been relatively short-lived initiatives funded on a time-limited basis.

2. *An ad-hoc, programme- and project-based approach to community practice:* Many change initiatives consist of centrally devised, 'off-the-shelf' programmes and projects. Imposed from the top, the credibility of such programmes is often questioned by the managers who are required to implement them – they find it difficult to see how they answer the real-life problems they have to address on a day-to-day basis. Too often they appear as 'yet another change initiative' in an apparently endless series, 'the meaning of each having long since become detached from their originator's intentions' (Wilkinson and Appelbee, 1999, p 36).

3. *An inward-looking, 'silo' mentality:* The immediate pressures of operational activity tend to limit the capacity and scope for broader based strategic thinking and planning. The outcome tends to be the

'enclosing' of the organisation, rather than opening it up to public discourse where the need for change can be expressed and discussed (Carly and Kirk, 2005). This tendency can extend to the separate departments and sections of the organisation – the so-called 'silo' tendency, where 'managerial attention is focused on internal silos to the detriment of a coherent approach to stakeholder needs' (Attwood et al, 2003, p 112).

4. *A value placed on organisational continuity; institutional memory underpins 'how we do things around here':* Research shows that public service organisations easily become absorbed in the requirements of continuity; services have to be provided in response to demands, often against the backcloth of reduced funding and resources; targets have to be met in response to the organisation's priorities and increasing central government pressures. In such an environment, these forces can work against positive and productive change. As already noted, organisations often retain an 'institutional memory' for certain patterns of relationships and organisational processes, and these make discussing and processing change difficult. The expectations of local authorities and other public organisations become subject to rigidification by a history of past actions and practices.

   Choosing health (Department of Health, 2004) and the *Delivering race equality action plan* (Department of Health, 2003) are two particular policies that reflect this feature. These policies promote, and provide some new resources for, community practice activity. However, traditional ways of seeing and doing things are often creating barriers to implementation that are proving difficult to overcome.

5. *A focus on operational issues and contingencies:* A further criticism of 'programmatic' change effort is that it is often primarily directed at the symptoms of the latest problem or moral panic. Such change efforts are frequently 'directed at tackling the presenting problem rather than aimed at the underlying causes' (Attwood et al, 2003, p 6).

6. *A corporate 'professional-bureaucratic' model of organisation and service provision:* Involving community members in developing services, projects and programmes may be an increasing requirement, but its realisation remains minimal in many cases. Its implementation is often criticised for being 'tokenistic', a necessary part of 'ticking the boxes' exercises to ensure continued funding. Local community representation, 'for example in Local Strategic Partnerships, often

amounts to only 3 or 4 people' (Macmillan and Townsend, 2006, p 20).

7. *An overwhelming sense of bombardment from the number, range and complexity of political, policy and bureaucratic demands made on community-based policy and programmes:* Such a sense can be experienced as the combined result of the points highlighted above, but this also brings about a further negative consequence – an attitude of resigned, half-hearted, and sometimes almost 'ritualistic', compliance in the face of unachievable demands: 'many people in organisations are drowning in the flood of bureaucracy from above, which results in compliance to meaningless number chasing and a low trust culture' (Attwood et al, 2003, p 16).

Organisational leadership and management: what needs to change?

Identifying the problematic features of contemporary community practice in this way offers some pointers to how such weaknesses can be addressed (see Figure 6.2). The remainder of this chapter advances an argument that three interrelated step-changes in the way organisational management and leadership for community practice is approached offer at least some potential for addressing such weaknesses in an effective way.

In Figure 6.2 the challenges and problems noted above are listed in the left-hand column, and alongside them is presented a list of what needs to change.

An inspection of the right-hand column reveals a number of common themes about what needs to change. Three in particular stand out. They are each mentioned more than once, are apparently based on similar assumptions, and seem to be consistent with the other responses. These are:

- the need for an increase in systems thinking and action;
- the need for a greater stress on organisational learning; and
- the need to adopt a 'distributed' form of leadership.

Our basic proposition is that new thinking is required if the contemporary weaknesses of organisational management and leadership of community practice are to be addressed. Such thinking focuses on how organisational managers might, with profit, modify how they think about and work on issues of organisational culture, organisational learning, and organisational leadership. Taken together, the results of

Figure 6.2: Addressing the problems and weaknesses of organisational management of community practice

Organisational management of community practice – challenges, problems and weaknesses	*Addressing the problems and weaknesses requires organisational management of community practice to:*
1. a reactive, 'fire-fighting' approach, 'short-termism';	1. establish 'strategic' approaches to sustainable long-term change; look to long-term, sustainable and strategic approaches, rather than the 'quick fix';
2. ad-hoc, project- and programme-based approaches to community practice – a 'top-down, target driven, inspection heavy quest for big solutions';	2. adopt whole-systems approach to planning and implementing community practice; resist fragmented and 'one-size-fits-all' approaches;
3. an insular and inward-looking organisational stance; the 'silo' mentality;	3. become outward looking – working in partnership with all stakeholders (community members and/or their representatives, as well as private, voluntary organisations, and other (statutory) agencies that represent wider public interests); encourage diversity of local solutions, based on local knowledge and preferences;
4. a value placed on organisational continuity: this is based on institutional memory about 'how we do things around here'; deeply entrenched in patterns of relationships and organisational processes;	4. promote a 'change-orientated' culture based on values and ideals (particularly democratic decision making), along with the dispositions (particularly those associated with 'learning as a way of being') of 'critical consciousness';
5. a focus on operational issues and contingencies;	5. develop organisational capacity for broader-based strategic systems thinking, along with new models of shared leadership;
6. a corporate 'professional-bureaucratic' model of service provision; policies and plans devised by policy makers/politicians, implemented by bureau-professionals;	6. develop 'empowering' models of organisational planning and delivery, engaging active citizens in leadership positions at all levels;
7. an overwhelming sense of 'bombardment' by the number, range and complexity of political and policy demands for community-based policy and programmes, 1997–2006 (the 'policy nightmare').	7. adopt a principle-based systems 'framework for action' capable of rationalising, prioritising and coordinating, and, therefore, better coping with the barrage of policy imperatives.

such modifications offer the possibility of step-change improvement in the support and facilitation of community practice in general and critical community practice in particular.

Figure 6.3 represents organisational culture, organisational learning and organisational leadership diagrammatically as three 'systems', each of which has an important influence on the functioning of a fourth system – which, in the diagram, is called the 'management action' system. Each component in the model will be discussed in turn, along with illustrations drawn from the case examples of critical community practice presented in Chapter Three, as appropriate.

An introductory comment on the 'management action system' in Figure 6.3 may be helpful before going further. This system comprises the week-by-week functions and tasks of those who carry responsibility for the organisational management of critical community practice. Such functions and tasks have been described in conventional terms, as 'setting strategic direction', 'organising', 'coordination and control', and so forth. While these terms are in common currency (and are seen as the 'bread and butter' functions of management in many general texts on organisational management), the particular way they are interpreted and handled in practice, we argue, will be significantly conditioned

Figure 6.3: Critical community practice: organisational systems

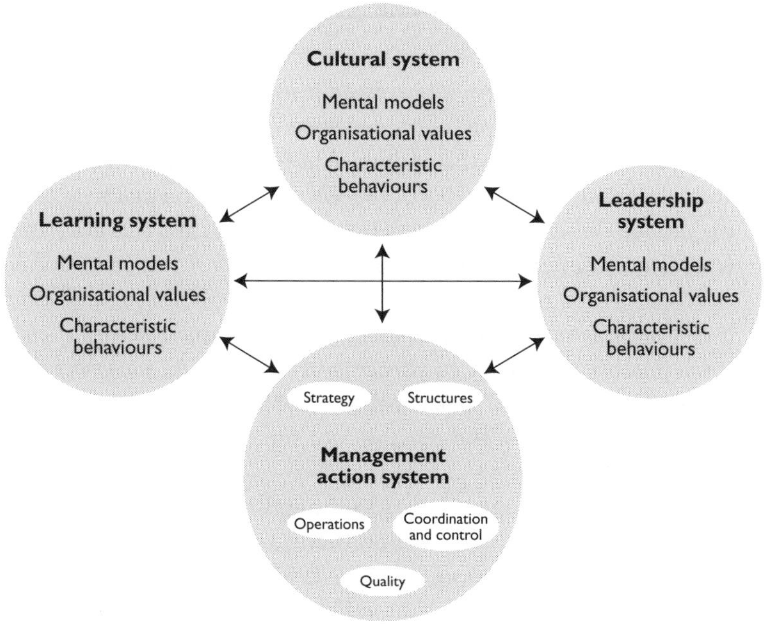

by the beliefs, values and behaviours that constitute the other three elements of the model, thereby shaping the character of organisational management and leadership for critical practice. We return to these connections later in the chapter.

Organisational culture

Organisational culture is now acknowledged by managers, academic commentators and researchers to play a vital role in how, and how effectively, organisations operate. An organisation's culture can affect, for example, the process and focus of its strategic planning, the way in which its work operations are organised and coordinated, its stance towards other organisations in its operating environment, and how it recruits, rewards and develops its staff. Nevertheless, it is sometimes difficult to 'pin down', precisely, what is meant when reference is made to organisational culture, or to articulate with any exactitude how the culture of organisation X might be said to differ from that of organisation Y. Managers sometimes refer to the mission, vision and values of their organisation as a way of illustrating what they mean by culture (Sadler, 1995) and researchers have attempted to draw up sets of continua along which the cultures of different organisations may be differentiated and compared (Hofstede, 2003; Trompenaars, 1997).

A useful way of unpacking the concept of organisational culture and illustrating its relevance is to think about it in terms of three interlinked components.

- *'Mental models'*: this term is borrowed from Peter Senge who defines mental models as 'deeply ingrained assumptions, generalisations, or even pictures or images that influence how we understand the world and take action' (Senge, 1990, p 8). We construct mental models all the time in our efforts to make sense of our world and our place in it. It was noted, for example, in Chapter Four that critical practitioners envisage (that is, operate with a mental model of) society and social institutions as socially constructed, and that human beings possess some potential to jointly construct (and reconstruct) aspects of their social relationships and social institutions. Such beliefs will influence, in turn, their view of the dynamics of the organisation they work in and/or manage.
- *'Core principles' (or values)*: refers to those things that 'organisational members collectively see as important and which consequently tend to guide their actions' (Sadler, 1995, p 28). The cooperative enterprises described in Chapter Three had signed up to a set of

principles drawn up by Cooperatives UK (the central membership organisation for cooperative enterprises throughout the UK). These included principles of self-responsibility, democracy, equality, equity, and solidarity, and were held to be underpinned by organisational ideals such as voluntary and open membership, democratic member control, and sustainable community development.

- *'Characteristic behaviours'*: refers to normative forms of organisational behaviour – 'how we do things around here' – and can include anything from expectations about dress codes, how people relate to each other, and how decisions are made.

With these distinctions in mind, we can turn to issues of organisational culture with reference to organisational management and leadership of critical community practice.

Mental models: 'systems thinking' and 'whole-systems approaches' to change: Figure 6.2 pointed to the importance of: adopting holistic approaches to planning and implementing community practice; working in partnership with all relevant stakeholders (community members and/or their representatives, as well as private, voluntary organisations, and other (statutory) agencies that represent wider public interests); and developing their organisational capacity for long-term strategic thinking and action. Attwood et al (2003) provide a clear account of how systems thinking and whole-systems action works and can make a real difference to practice in this area. A systems approach to managing critical community practice invites us to consider the neighbourhoods, estates and villages that comprise a locality community as 'systems'– systems moreover that operate alongside and engage in reciprocal relations with a number of other systems (local regeneration and other support agencies, the business sector, the local political system, a range of local government and other service and administrative agencies and charitable bodies, and so on). A systems approach holds that complex, so-called 'messy' and 'wicked' issues – such as urban blight and decline, social exclusion, or homelessness – are influenced by action taken (or not taken) by a host of agencies, professional workers and community organisations – and it is only rarely that any one of those agencies can hope to 'fix' such problems on their own. An individual agency may try to go it alone, drawing upon its own 'programmatic' change solutions, often by deploying a mechanistic approach based on organisational re-engineering, or rationalising the programmes it has responsibility for, within its own 'silo'. The 'problem' is broken down into its component elements and change strategies are designed 'top-down' (and with reference to the organisations' own remit and resources), and then rolled out to achieve the necessary changes. But such strategies rarely make the problem go away – it keeps on coming round.

> We reasoned that it might be more fruitful to think of them (i.e. such 'wicked' problems) as issues for an interconnected system to tackle together … shifting attention from the parts to the whole, and thus to the connections between parts – and how things fit together. (Pratt et al, 2005, p 1)

This quasi-organic notion – of an adaptive 'social ecology' of interdependent systems – helps us to think of individuals, teams, departments, communities and organisations as purposeful entities linked together in webs or networks of interdependence and interconnectedness, capable of devising (through the combined intelligence and coordinated efforts of each constituent part), multi-organisational responses to multi-faceted problems. The action strategies that derive from a 'mental model' of whole-systems working are usefully reviewed in Attwood et al (2003) and Pratt et al (2005).

Core principles: 'stakeholder involvement' and 'sustainable development' as core organisational principles: These two principles were seen to be central to critical community practice in Chapters Three and Four. Figure 6.2 likewise stresses the importance of looking to long-term, sustainable and strategic approaches (rather than a 'quick fix'), through developing a transformative 'change-oriented' culture, underpinned by the ideals of participatory decision making.

The adoption of whole-systems thinking and joined-up change strategies will almost certainly go some way to achieving the goal of sustainable change. Implementation of holistic strategies is not easy, and takes time, but it is increasingly recognised that multi-organisational, partnership solutions have the best chance of achieving long-term change where intractable multi-faceted problems are concerned. As Senge argues, 'The systems viewpoint is generally oriented towards the long-term view' (1990, p 92).

Equally important, however, is a second factor: achieving maximum stakeholder engagement – in particular, the involvement of those who are directly experiencing the problem and issues under consideration. In all the case examples described in Chapter Three those with a direct personal 'stake' in each initiative (as householders, young people, parents of school-aged children, and so on) took a central role in both the long-term planning and the week-by-week implementation of the resultant community initiatives. It was their personal, long-term, engagement in problem solving (drawing on their direct day-to-day experience of the problem), and their committed involvement to jointly seeing through the initiatives and ensuring they 'worked' in their local context, that ensured the initial viability of the programme in the first place as well as its continuing effectiveness over the longer term.

'How we do things around here': commitment to joint action, supported by open communication, and shared understanding: A key basis on which community practice initiatives are developed and run appears to be the growth of a kind of 'instrumental' solidarity – a commitment, through shared experience, through conversation and deliberation on shared circumstances and conditions, to build a joint understanding of the dynamics of long-standing problems which help to develop the commitment and energy to drive forward change.

Organisational learning

Organisational learning, the second system discussed here, complements and reinforces the approach to organisational culture outlined above. A particular model of great relevance to effective critical community practice is outlined, before moving on to discuss core principles, and then characteristic 'learning' behaviours.

Mental model: 'experiential action–learning': We gave considerable attention to questions of learning when identifying the key components of the model of 'critical community practice' in Chapter Four. The kind of learning seen as foundational to 'critical consciousness' put relatively little stress on institutionally based study (via courses, workshops and other formal learning in educational establishments) and gave much more emphasis to recognising the importance of, and refining the practice of learning from, experience. David Kolb's (1984) cyclical theory of experiential learning offers a four-stage picture of how an individual learns from experience. The learning cycle begins

1. when the individual's attention is drawn to a particular aspect of their concrete experience (something that is, perhaps, unexpected, or difficult, or paradoxical), which
2. prompts a process of 'reflective observation' about the issue, which can, in turn, lead to

3. the construction of a hypothesis or 'theory' to make sense of what has been brought to their attention. Kolb calls this latter process 'abstract conceptualisation' – and it involves the learner in trying to relate or conceptualise their new experience with reference to their existing mental models and meaning structures. This can then lead to

4. 'active experimentation' in which new understandings are tested out through taking action, thereby confirming or disconfirming the learner's new knowledge.

The assumptions behind Kolb's model are clearly consistent with those underpinning the critical community practice model; they embrace a constructionist view of learning, seeing knowledge creation as an active interpretive process – one, moreover, that takes place in a whole series of iterative cycles that accords well with the notion of lifelong learning, and learning as a 'way of being'.

Nancy Dixon (1994) builds on Kolb's model by expanding it to cover more than just individual learning. Organisational learning (and other forms of collective learning) is more than the sum of an individual member's personal learning. When personal meaning structures (for example, our 'mental models') are disclosed and discussed with colleagues then shared 'collective' meaning structures can be constructed, group perspectives can evolve, and the validity of collective organisational knowledge can potentially be sifted and evaluated, and suggested modifications to organisational practice can be checked out in practice. If effective – then such modifications can be rolled out for wider adoption within the organisation. In short, the organisation can be said to have learned. Nevis et al (1995) identify the processes that will advance such organisational learning:

- refinement of processes through which people at all levels in the organisation can acquire and develop new knowledge and perspectives;
- development of processes through which such knowledge and perspectives can confidently be disclosed, disseminated, shared and discussed with other organisational members;
- putting in place processes through which the validity and usefulness of new knowledge can be sifted and evaluated in the light of their potential contributions to organisational improvement; and, finally,

- adoption of processes through which proposed improvements can be checked, trialled, and – if effective – rolled out for wider adoption within the organisation (Butcher and Robertson, 2003).

When such a model of learning is deployed within a whole-systems framework (with all key stakeholders engaging in processes of debate and constructive dialogue), organisational learning begins to demonstrate its potential for critical community practice.

Core principle: 'learning as a way of being': 'Public', and inclusive, experiential learning in an organisation enables 'learning as a way of being' (Chapter Four) to develop as a core principle. We saw in Chapter Three how exercises in participatory community governance – involvement in, for example, local participatory budgeting or cooperative housing management – can become a vehicle for powerful and continuous learning, including development of organisational and political skills and knowledge, as well as changes in attitudes and values, and enhancement of self-esteem and a sense of personal efficacy.

How we do things around here: 'conversations with a purpose' and 'public' learning: Learning organisations are characterised by providing the opportunities, and putting in place the mechanisms that facilitate, 'public learning'. 'Conversations with a purpose' are supported, for example, through action-learning sets, whole-system conferencing, quality circles, facilitative leadership of team learning, opening up channels of transparent organisational communications both vertically and horizontally, and e-based discussion groups that support 'communities of practice'.

Organisational leadership

Organisational leadership faces new challenges as charismatic and 'heroic' notions of leadership (the so-called 'John Wayne school of leadership'), as well as the autocratic 'command and control' styles of leadership to be found in 'machine bureaucracies', are replaced by newer forms of 'shared' and 'empowered' leadership (Bolden, 2004). Here we focus on the model 'distributed leadership' and then turn, once again, to core principles and characteristic behaviours.

- *Mental model; 'distributed leadership':* Advocacy of a 'one best way' approach to leadership has fewer and fewer adherents – diversity in organisational contexts, tasks and time-lines lend support to 'contingency' approach to leadership.

The 'distributive' model of leadership sits comfortably with the values and ethos of working methods of critical community practice. Rather than view leadership as a function of the personality of the leader, or as a derivative of their organisational status and position, it can be conceptualised as a type of *activity*, and draw on insights from recent advances in activity theory. Diamond (2006) invites us to consider an analogy with the flight deck on an aeroplane to illustrate the fundamental point of activity theory:

> Think of the cockpit of the airplane – the people in the cockpit, the instrument panel, the people who are trying to help the plane land – and try to think about the activity of landing the plane not as something an individual person does, not as something the instrument panel does without the people, not as something a pilot could do without the air traffic controller. Try to think about the whole activity system. (Diamond, 2006, p 1)

This concept of leadership has been pioneered by Spillane (2006) in his studies of school principals in Chicago. The increasing responsibility given to, and the complexity of the demands made on, these school leaders has rendered traditional models of principalship outmoded. Even the most capable and highly qualified principal will not have the skills and time at their disposal to master the increasingly complex agenda that the contemporary high school has to address.

Principals have found that they need to 'distribute' leadership (for curriculum development, pastoral care, estates, and so forth) to key colleagues throughout the organisation. This is not to be confused with delegation – it constitutes a 'division of (leadership) labour', with those who lead being those with the optimum expertise and experience to co-produce the leadership 'function' required within the organisation. Reviewing the literature on distributed leadership, Bennett et al (2003) identify a range of issues and challenges that influence the success or otherwise of distributed leadership: for example, the importance of high levels of organisational (or inter-organisational, if we are thinking of partnership working) trust, and strong shared goals; ensuring the right balance between control and autonomy within the leadership team; and the rigidity or malleability of existing leadership traditions in particular settings.

While it is not an easy option, distributed leadership has much to offer organisations that support critical community practice. It is, above all, an approach that can draw on the range of expertise and talents that become available to, and necessary for the success of, whole-systems working. At the same time it demonstrates a good 'fit' with the participatory aspirations of critical practice, particularly if it is complemented by Senge's 'new' view of leadership, which focuses on the roles of leaders as organisational 'designers', 'stewards' and 'teachers' (Senge, 1990, p 340).

- *Core principle:* A fruitful alignment exists between distributed leadership and the egalitarian aspirations of critical practice. Hofstede (1991) has noted that organisations vary along a dimension he calls 'power-difference'; distributed leadership will encourage low emphasis on status differentials and the formalities of rank, and put a premium on open communications and participative and inclusive approaches to decision making.

- *'How we do things around here':* Leadership as an 'activity' means that it is likely to have a 'fluid' feel about it. Those offering leadership will change, and possibly rotate, over time as circumstances alter, and as the capacities and skills of different organisational members meet the requirements of particular pieces of work.

Implications for management action

This overview of systems working, organisational learning and distributed leadership has incorporated a number of illustrations of working with such systems in the context of community practice.

We now return to review, a little more systematically, the operational consequences of these systems for selected aspects of the 'management action system' (Figure 6.3). We will focus here on the management functions of strategic planning, organisational structure and co-ordination and control for illustrative purposes.

Strategic planning: A variety of approaches to developing organisational strategy have been developed over recent decades; Johnson and Scholes (2003), for example, identify the following: visionary, planning, political, cultural, and logical-incrementalist views.

The logical-incrementalist view has, in particular, much to offer strategic planning within a whole-systems perspective. Henry Mintzberg (1989, 1994) drawing on research by Lindblom (1968) and others has persuasively argued that organisational strategy is best viewed as something that develops over time, as a sequence of incremental adjustments to organisational goals and practices, designed to achieve progressively a more effective alignment between aspirational goals, environmental constraints and actual achievements to date. While it may be feasible for key decision makers of relevant agencies to come together in order to reach a consensual overview of joint strategic intentions, this will do little to encourage the general development of organisational relationships of trust, respect and mutual understanding that has been shown, in a number of research studies (Gilchrist, 2003), to be crucial to the day-to-day joint working at operational levels that are so important to long-term, sustainable partnership working. Nor will elitist, top-down approaches develop the learning capacity necessary for authentic grass-roots citizen involvement in key decision making. Whole-systems working, progressed over time via logical-incrementalist methods, allows organisational players to modify and develop their practice through a continuing series of mutual adjustments with their partners and stakeholders. Shared strategic vision and joint working often advance hand in hand; and the experiential learning cycle enables 'shared meaning structures' to evolve alongside joint, participative action, resulting in integrated sustainable solutions.

Organisational structures: Such an approach to strategic development will lay the foundations for team-based and network forms of organisation. Team-based (as opposed to bureaucratic, 'club', or loose-coupled) forms of organisation (Handy, 1985) operate through project teams and network systems, staffed and resourced according to the requirements of a time-defined project, and within the overall parameters of an evolving strategic vision. Charles Handy uses the metaphor of a 'net' when considering team-based organisation, with the work-teams constituting cells at the interstices of the net. Such structures are generally supportive environments for staff to work in and, help to break down departmentalism and 'silo' thinking, and flat team-based modes of organising facilitate distributive leadership. Finally, teams, with their task-driven culture (and membership selected accordingly), bring together personnel with a diversity of skills, perspectives and values – all of which creates a fertile soil for team and organisational learning.

Organisational coordination and control may appear, at first sight, to be more than usually problematic in such team-based, network-structured organisations. The importance of integrated planning and joined-up operations has been stressed; but surely this requires the utilisation of more bureaucratic control mechanisms, of a type that emphasises direct supervision (of workers, by line managers), an underlying preference for standardisation (of work processes and work outputs), along with the ability to exercise control through target setting, benchmarking and implementation of closely focused quality control procedures?

To suggest that there are no satisfactory alternatives to adopting such bureaucratic processes would, however, be a mistake. First, community practice processes and contexts render direct supervision of work processes virtually impossible, with standardisation of outputs only feasible at the most general level (Butcher and Robertson, 2003, p 78). Community practitioners, operating in fluid and complex operating environments, rely on an 'inner compass' of values and knowledge to plan and orientate their activities. The answer, then, is not to seek to ensure coordination and control through bureaucratic procedures. Rather, ensuring that the 'inner compass' is properly calibrated and functions well – through good initial and continuing work-based education and training – complemented by rigorous individual and team-based reflection, will be the most effective guarantor of high quality work processes and effective delivery of agreed outcomes.

Conclusions

We have argued that appropriate organisational management and leadership – no less than innovative policy making and effective face-to-face work in the community – is vitally important if the full potential offered by critical community practice is to be realised.

A step-change, it has been suggested, is urgently required in terms of organisational leadership and management of community practice. Such change will only be fully successful, however, if it is pursued across the board in 'whole-systems' terms. To continue to deploy current – weak and problematic – approaches, as critiqued at the beginning of the chapter, will continue to result in a failure to optimise 'active citizenship for social change'.

Limitation of space does not allow a comprehensive discussion of all the organisational systems that advocacy of a 'whole-systems' approach properly deserves. We have, therefore, focused on selected theoretical perspectives – related to the crucial systems of organisational culture, learning and leadership – sketching out some of the implications of these for organisational strategy, organisational structure and organisational coordination and control.

SEVEN

Politics and policy: a critical community practice perspective

Paul Henderson

In Chapter Six we underlined the extent to which local authorities, other public service organisations and large voluntary organisations face numerous and complex challenges. We now place the challenges in a broader context in order, first, to throw light on the capacity of these organisations to control and handle programmes and initiatives and, second, to use the model of critical community practice to suggest some of the implications of the wider political and policy context. Does the model extend to the political and policy contexts? How can it be used at this level?

We begin by sketching the global canvas as it relates to critical community practice before setting out the main developments and trends in UK politics and policy, focusing especially on community involvement and partnership policies. In the final section of the chapter we use the critical community practice model to discuss the connections with the politics and policies summarised.

Civil society

In 1994 a group of enthusiasts in Hungary founded a Civil College, based in a former primary school in an isolated rural area in the middle of the country. It is used as a training and conference centre for a wide range of non-governmental organisations (NGOs) and statutory organisations, as well as for international seminars. Throughout its history its focus has been – and continues to be – on engaging with key questions about civil society. What does the concept mean? How can it be brought to life for different interest groups and organisations? Above all, how does it relate to debates and concerns about democracy?

The Civil College in Hungary has a presence in a community setting – it employs local people, and is used by local groups and organisations. It is kept going through the commitment and 'sweat equity' of a handful of individuals and groups. Transferring these characteristics to the wider context, the setting up of the Civil College can be envisaged as a symbol or metaphor for wider study and discussion of the concept of civil society. This is particularly appropriate because, from a UK perspective, it was the role of civil society organisations in bringing to an end the communist regimes in Eastern and Central Europe that brought a key aspect of the concept of civil society to life. Today the concept has widespread global currency but from the early 1970s to the end of the 1980s it meant social movements that provided a serious and effective challenge to undemocratic regimes and that campaigned for a new kind of society, as pointed out by Marjorie Mayo:

> The case for building and maintaining a strong civil society has been put forward because this has been seen as providing a bulwark for democracy, limiting the potentially excessive powers of the state. This argument was used to justify programmes to strengthen civil society in Eastern and Central Europe, post-1989, just as similar arguments have been used to support the development of more decentralised and more participatory approaches to development in the South, with correspondingly enhanced roles for NGOs and community-based organisations. (Mayo, 2005, p 45)

As well as being used by NGOs, trade unions, churches and others in this social movement sense, the concept of civil society has been embraced by numerous other organisations:

> It appears in the reports and projects of the European Commission, the UN and the World Bank as well as in the programmes of political parties, governments and multinational firms ... Civil society relates in this way to the public sphere – to a defined manner and mentality as well as to the community of NGOs. This expanded usage preserves the ambiguity of the notion. It can serve to fight political battles, to mantle social and political problems, but can also turn into the language of power. (Jensen and Miszlivetz, 2003, p 45)

It is important to appreciate the profound significance that has been attached to the concept of civil society by activists and others in Eastern and Central Europe – even if the realities of many people who had great hopes of the revolutions have been very different to their dreams. It is also essential, however, to be alert to how it is used in other contexts.

This sense of commitment and passion associated with the concept does not exist in the West. It is still possible, for example, to attend conferences in the UK where the concepts of civil society and civic society are used interchangeably. This is unhelpful and misleading: the idea of civic society – the municipal civic centre, the active citizen in the context of the government's civil renewal programmes – has to be understood within the wider domain of civil society. In a sense, the former is dependent for its meaning and effectiveness on the vibrancy and strength of the latter. The case studies in Chapter Three demonstrate how democratic power can be exercised with civil society, providing a counter-balance to state power. Grasping the importance of the fundamental political nature of civil society, especially the capacity of ordinary people to organise themselves in ways that bring them into dialogue with, and/or challenge, the state is necessary for our discussion of critical community practice.

Social capital

Equally powerful as the concept of civil society in the global context is that of social capital, albeit for different reasons. Its origins lie in research and in that sense it is a 'top-down' concept that has been picked up enthusiastically by a wide range of politicians and policy makers. The literature mostly uses a three-fold definition of social capital:

- *bonding:* based on enduring, multi-faceted relationships between similar people with strong mutual commitments such as among friends, family and other close-knit groups;
- *bridging:* formed from the connections between people who have less in common, but may have an overlapping interest, for example, between neighbours, colleagues, or between different groups within a community;
- *linking:* derived from the links between people or organisations beyond peer boundaries, cutting across status and similarity and enabling people to exert influence and reach resources outside their normal circles (Gilchrist, 2004, p 6).

Social capital too can be found in the policy statements of international agencies. The World Bank's Social Capital Initiative has analysed systematically the literature on social capital. A report of the Organisation for Economic Co-operation and Development (OECD) promotes the idea that social capital, or the benefits of strong community ties and social networks, can contribute to well-being and economic growth.

The report also makes the point that, while social capital is informal and organic by its very nature, public policy can be instrumental in encouraging it; the report urges social capital to be measured and promoted (OECD, 2001).

It cannot be assumed that the way in which the concepts of civil society and social capital are used by inter-governmental organisations and national politicians is shared necessarily by community activists and non-governmental organisations who, in general, look for very 'grounded' definitions:

> The development of trust and reciprocity is seen as a critical foundation of programmes aimed at the eradication of poverty. However, the concept of social capital risks being treated as a panacea for all social problems. If we want to draw on the strengths of social capital we need a clear understanding of how this concept operates. (Hautekeur, 2005, p 16)

This is relevant to our discussion of critical community practice: evidence as to the importance of social capital can lend weight to the need to have properly resourced community practice programmes but the policy makers and programme managers must take seriously two points: they should support and facilitate, not control, the growth of social capital and they must be aware that the concept is as important for community groups and networks committed to strengthening their communities as it is for policy makers. The latter do not have a monopoly of how the concept is used:

> Public policy will have to learn how to strengthen support for this activity without co-opting it either into party politics or into the language and accountability structures of public service professionals. (Skidmore and Craig, 2005, p 14)

An example of applying social capital theory within a broader framework of the health and well-being of society is provided by Wilkinson's use of the concept in the context of health inequality. He argues that people in developed countries have become increasingly aware of the contrast between the material success and social failure of modern societies, and he questions the dominance of economic growth as a societal goal:

> In its place we must operationalise values of human social
> and material emancipation, ensuring that narrower income
> differences extend dignity to all and so provide a material
> base conducive to the proper development of the social life
> of our societies. (Wilkinson, 1996, p 222)

Wilkinson uses the research undertaken on social capital to support his
arguments on inequalities in health: people with good social networks
live longer than those with poor networks.

We have selected the concepts of civil society and social capital to
draw attention to the extent of the competing and complex themes
that exist in the global context. In addition to health inequality, they
extend to other major issues: environmental conditions, social exclusion
and economically disadvantaged communities. We believe that critical
community practice needs to engage with this global context, otherwise
it will be in danger of becoming inward-looking and starved of ideas
and experiences.

Politics and policy

The extent to which the representative political system is in crisis
has been a subject of debate by politicians, political theorists and
commentators for more than 15 years. It is a debate that is taking
place in many societies. However, at this point we shall focus on the
UK. There has been a growing stream of publications, some based
on research, some on political and social analysis. In the mid-1990s,
for example, *The Political Quarterly* journal published a collection of
essays on the vulnerability of democracy in Western Europe: 'The need
for a new agenda of democratic politics, as well as for new vigour in
prosecuting it, is very clear in the British case' (Hirst and Khilnani, 1996,
p 1). This viewpoint reflected the widespread concern about the future
of democracy in Britain. It was an important theme, for example, in the
report of the Commission on Social Justice, set up at the instigation of
John Smith, then Leader of the Labour Party:

> The challenge is to develop new mechanisms of collective
> action which will at the same time meet common goals
> and liberate individual talent. Far from living through the
> death of politics, we depend on its resurrection for national
> renewal. (Commission on Social Justice, 1994, p 98)

As Hugh Butcher comments in Chapter Four, disaffection with the representative political system has become ever stronger. Membership of political parties has fallen significantly and in the 2005 general election more people chose not to vote (39 per cent) than voted for the governing Labour party. The word 'crisis' is used regularly to describe the current disengagement of the public from political activity and decline in trust in government:

> Our politics duck the big and difficult issues like climate change and pensions reform but at the same time seems unable to put right even small things. So it is not just new leaders, but a new democratic settlement, that we need – a paradigm shift in the way we do democracy. (Bentley, 2005, p 5)

The issue of political disengagement can be discussed from various perspectives. Here we look at it first from a grass-roots and then from a policy 'think-tank' perspective. Traditionally, community development has often exposed the raw nerve lying between campaigning community groups and local councillors. All too frequently there is a strong sense of distance between the two, particularly when one of the main political parties has a near monopoly of people's votes. Do similar tensions exist today between activists and councillors or has the introduction of partnership boards and forums had the effect of taking the sting out of the relationship?

Arguably, the problem has been compounded by the trend for backbench councillors to be absorbed into the organisational procedures of local authorities. The government's proposals, contained in its White Paper *Strong and prosperous communities* (Department for Communities and Local Government, 2006), for local authorities to decentralise their operations and to initiate neighbourhood management, and for greater involvement of local communities in making decisions about services, will hopefully begin to reverse this trend. Indeed, some local authorities have demonstrated a determination to try out new approaches to citizens' involvement; Blackburn with Darwen Borough Council, for example, set up a social change project to involve more than 400 residents, using learning methods pioneered by Freire. Subsequently, this Neighbourhood Learning Planning project was included in government programmes aimed at sharing best practice among local authorities (Yarnit, 2005).

It seems likely, however, that initiatives and programmes designed to take forward the concept of governance, a bringing together of representative and participatory democracy, will need to work hard to break down the attitudes of many local people towards their locally elected representatives. These often combine cynicism and anger. They can also reflect frustration at what they perceive to be inadequate performances by councillors – a feeling that local activists could fulfil the role better. It is not just in hard-pressed urban areas where these views can be found. For example, the final report on the Countryside Agency's Community Development Worker programme included the following finding:

> There are indications from the Community Development Worker reports that some community members, having played an active role in a community project, are getting elected to Parish Councils. The motivation for this action is often provoked by the failure of the Parish Council to support a local initiative or sometimes where it has specifically raised objections or barriers to community plans. Activists are then driven to seek to bring about change from within the democratic structure and process. (Community Development Foundation, 2005, p 45)

Being able to access information about plans for communities and the opportunities for community involvement is also an issue from the grass-roots perspective. The widespread availability of government and other policy papers on websites does not deal with this issue at a stroke. The report of a community research process undertaken in Bradford on the views of Black and Minority Ethnic mental health service users on participation in the NHS illustrates the point. Entitled *Participation... Why bother?* the conclusion drawn from five community workshops involving 63 people was that the biggest barrier was 'the belief that the health service will not listen, and that change won't follow' (Blakey, 2005, p 4). Other barriers included the power structures within the system and a lack of information. The example reminds us that the issue of political disengagement is, as far as local people are concerned, about a cluster of problems, some to do with locally elected members and some with organisational and information barriers. Between 2001 and 2003 the Home Office's citizenship survey showed that fewer people thought they had any influence over the decisions affecting their local areas – a fall from 43 per cent to 38 per cent.

The experiences of political disengagement of local people and campaigning groups, along with the flow of academic research findings, have prompted a number of think-tanks to investigate the issue. Demos,

Charter 88, the New Politics Network, the Institute for Public Policy Research and others have all initiated research and policy work with the aim of stimulating public debate. This was certainly the intention of the Power Inquiry, which is an independent group funded by two of the Rowntree trusts and chaired by Helena Kennedy QC. The inquiry aimed to explore how political participation and involvement might be increased and deepened in Britain. In doing so, it set out a devastating critique of the state of formal democracy in the country, based on a number of explanations (summarised by Hugh Butcher in Chapter Four). The inquiry's report argues strongly that this cannot be explained by public apathy. It identifies the problem as the decline in formal politics, pointing out that large numbers of people are engaged in community and charity work outside of politics:

> There is also clear evidence that involvement in pressure politics – such as signing petitions, supporting consumer boycotts, joining campaign groups – has been growing significantly for many years. In addition, research shows that interest in 'political issues' is high. (Power Inquiry, 2006, p 16)

It can be seen that there is, to some extent, a disjunction between this viewpoint and the grass-roots analysis given earlier: while there is agreement on the overriding problem, the Power Inquiry puts forward a more optimistic profile of public interest in issues compared with our understanding of the experiences of community groups. The inquiry, however, makes a powerful case for what it refers to as the need to 'download power' – the introduction of institutional and cultural changes that place a new emphasis on the requirement for policy and decision making to include rigorous and meaningful input from 'ordinary' citizens.

The Power report is an example of a group located within the progressive liberal tradition reaching conclusions which are similar to those being put forward by campaigning organisations and pressure groups. The significance of the Power Inquiry's analysis and recommendations has been acknowledged across the political spectrum. The ensuing debate, and the decision of the funders to continue the work of the inquiry in order that some of its recommendations can be taken forward, is perhaps an indication of the uncertainty and anxiety surrounding the contemporary political context

Government responses

To an extent, the Labour government has acknowledged this situation. When he first came to power, Tony Blair made evident his interest in communitarian ideas, particularly those put forward by the American sociologist Etzioni, which place an emphasis on the values of reciprocity, good neighbourliness and mutuality:

> Communitarianism is concerned with inculcating in ordinary people a sense of responsibility for their own well-being, the family and the community to which they belong. (Henderson and Salmon, 1998, p 24)

One can understand how, from the perspective of politicians and policy makers, such ideas would lead them to support the need for community involvement and partnership in regeneration and social inclusion programmes. Communitarianism provided a theoretical underpinning – albeit the theories on which it is based are contestable – for a series of community involvement and community engagement policies. Tony Blair was also drawn to the ideas covered by the term 'the Third Way', as conceptualised by Giddens, because of the strong message contained within it for the renewal of democracy:

> The theme of community is fundamental to the new politics, but not just as an abstract slogan. The advance of globalisation makes a community focus both necessary and possible, because of the downward pressure it exerts. 'Community' doesn't imply trying to recapture lost forms of solidarity; it refers to practical means of furthering the social and material refurbishment of neighbourhoods, towns and larger local areas. (Giddens, 1998, p 79)

Within this extract we can trace the links to the government's neighbourhood renewal, and other, programmes. For a number of years, Giddens was an adviser to the Prime Minister on democratic reform. In the Labour government's third term the prominence given by senior ministers to communitarian and Third Way ideas waned. Regeneration and other programmes, however, continued to emphasise the importance of community involvement. It had begun with the launch by the Prime Minister of the Social Exclusion Unit's first report on how to develop 'integrated and sustainable approaches' to social problems:

> Too much has been imposed from above when experience shows that success depends on communities themselves having the power and taking the responsibility to make things better. And although there are good examples of rundown neighbourhoods turning themselves around, the lessons haven't been learned properly. (Social Exclusion Unit, 1998, p 5)

We have here a strong critique of previous regeneration programmes because of their failure to involve communities. In the subsequent years the theme of community involvement has been integral to a wide range of neighbourhood renewal, sustainable development and social inclusion policies. In his review of community involvement and urban policy, Gabriel Chanan comments:

> Community involvement occupies a unique but somewhat puzzling position in current social policy. On the one hand it is a requirement accompanying virtually every policy to do with local governance and public services. On the other hand it is often vague or ambiguous in specific policy documents. (Chanan, 2003, p 15)

Analysing in detail what community involvement means in practice to all the participating organisations and groups of regeneration and other programmes will continue to be important. This is because of the generality or vagueness of the concept. The same judgement can be made of the term 'community engagement', which is widely used in the health sector: engagement on whose terms? At one national conference a participant asked the panel to explain the theoretical basis of the concept of community engagement and received the answer 'public relations'!

The example used by Connelly of a case study of public involvement in sustainable development work (Local Agenda 21) in a very traditional English local authority is the kind of material that is needed – data and insights which lead to fine grain analysis. The engagement of the community in this case was over-managed and very few local community groups or individuals became involved, leading the author to conclude that:

> Community representatives have to go beyond simply 'participating' and attempt to become more active players in the larger policy-making 'game': to recognise its strategic

nature and the different levels at which it is played, to form alliances with those with compatible and complementary goals in order to increase their leverage, and so to engage actively in designing, controlling and framing public involvement processes. (Connelly, 2006, p 22)

Closely linked with the community involvement requirement of regeneration funding programmes is the elevation of partnership to the overall policy framework. Whereas in the past partnership was seen to be desirable, for the last 15 years it has been laid down as an imperative. It underpins all planning and regeneration programmes: forums and boards – Local Strategic Partnerships (LSPs) in England being a most prominent example – on which all the sectors are represented. In Scotland, community planning is considered to be the overarching framework for inter-agency working to tackle social exclusion at the local level. Local authorities take the lead but they are expected to foster a climate of community involvement in decision making. Globally, 'Partnership has become the currency of policy-making in countries across the world' (Taylor, 2003, p 114).

The actual running of partnerships, particularly in the context of LSPs, has been criticised for lacking an understanding of the position of community participants: the pressures on their time, their need to keep in close contact with their constituencies and dealing with information overload. The checklist devised for LSPs by Rupa Sarkar and Alison West, which covers participative structure, the commitment of partners, the availability of training and the resources available for taking forward a community involvement plan is designed to deal with these problems (Sarkar and West, 2003, pp 18–19).

Despite problems still evident in much partnership working, the principle that interventions in communities should be planned and implemented on a partnership basis has broadly been welcomed. Partnerships can be mutually beneficial and create new opportunities: 'Partnership has put excluded groups and communities onto the agenda in a way that they have not been before' (Balloch and Taylor, 2001, p 286).

Crucial to their effectiveness is the availability and accessibility of training on the skills needed for partnership working: capacity building, networking and negotiation.

Applying the model

The number of examples of partnership projects across the UK and other parts of Europe which take community involvement seriously is growing. In both urban and rural areas local people, practitioners and managers are seeking to develop good practice in this crucially important sphere of community practice. Given the overall global context outlined at the beginning of this chapter, and the particular characteristics of public policy in the UK, the key question for our critical community practice model is, how can it be applied at the political and policy level? Does it extend to this dimension or is its application more evident in practice and organisational settings? There follow five suggestions as to how the model could be used in the political and policy context.

Political analysis

Funding and monitoring pressures on regeneration and social inclusion programmes are so all-consuming for those most directly involved that rigorous analysis of the surrounding local, regional and national politics is often neglected. It is not prioritised. It is also not a topic about which most people are experienced or confident. They cannot access concepts that are needed in order to undertake serious political analysis.

The critical community practice model can be used as a tool for this process. We are thinking especially of the concept of 'power with' discussed in Chapter Two: the scope it offers either to reduce a conflict situation or to move a project into a more secure, advantageous position in ways that do not disadvantage other 'players'. Developing a political analysis on this basis goes beyond good practice in partnership working because it requires there to be an accurate and sensitive assessment of where power lies and how apparently fixed attitudes can be changed. In such a setting the art of negotiation and the skills of listening and communicating are elevated to a higher level than is common for most managers, practitioners and community leaders. Essentially, using the model in this way is making explicit the importance of politics, rescuing it from the denigrated cul-de-sac where it is often perceived to lie.

When stakeholders engage in political analysis that draws upon key concepts of power, it is possible to demonstrate at the political and policy level the alternative power paradigms discussed in Chapter Two, not by being able to point to particular outputs or to organisational changes but through the clarification and articulation of key concepts. Accordingly, the model puts a premium here on the currency of ideas, sharpening and investigating them and setting them alongside each other.

Precedents for this emphasis on careful political analysis can be found in mediation and reconciliation approaches used to find common ground among protagonists in severe conflict situations, such as that which dominated Northern Ireland for so long. Skilled individuals who can facilitate dialogue are needed but so too are individuals and groups who have the clarity of purpose and the ability both to put forward and dissect arguments. This can only be achieved by investing in political analysis that draws upon such key concepts as civil society and social capital.

Identifying trends

The fast pace set by the Labour government since 1997 for its regeneration, planning, social inclusion and other programmes – one following another in rapid succession – has made it difficult for those involved in the programmes to track the ways things are moving: is local government reform actually happening? Are the criticisms of partnership working being addressed? What impact are capacity-building programmes having? Above all, what is happening to the relationship between communities and the state?

The critical community practice model is relevant here because of its emphasis on sharing and exploring developments among stakeholders and on distilling their 'lived' experiences. The model's usefulness lies in the contribution it can make to transformational social change; the essence of the contribution is its capacity to bring to the table a deciphering of what is happening within communities and state institutions, as well as the relationship between them. The model, in this sense, provides a framework for helping groups and organisations to find out where they are on the political and policy map. That can result in them being significantly better positioned: understanding the problem before moving to solutions.

Examples of how the model can be applied in this way can be found in the work of regional organisations in England that work on behalf of the voluntary and community sector. They need to be good at 'reading' the changing political scene at regional level by being in close contact with a region's government office, the regional development agency and the large local authorities. At the same time, they have to stay close to the voluntary and community sector in all its diversity because it is this which ultimately is the regional organisation's constituency. It is by operating in these ways that it can achieve an accurate assessment of political and policy trends.

Thus, identifying trends ceases to be the monopoly of statisticians and policy analysts. It becomes part of the work of those people and organisations directly or indirectly involved in programmes. The critical community practice model thereby lives up to its claim of being able to contribute to a different future.

Critiquing policies and practice

What do we mean by this? Essentially it is to do with searching behind the political statements and policy guidelines for the ideas which inform them. We are aware that engaging in this process will make explicit the ideological and value beliefs of individuals and possibly lead to the cut and thrust of disagreement and debate. This, we believe, is healthy because it places critical discussion of politics and policies in the mainstream rather than relegating it to the margins of public discourse and planning. It can be illustrated by the argument put forward by Marilyn Taylor and Mandy Wilson that higher priority needs to be given, at various levels, to neighbourhoods:

> Nowhere is the strategic link between neighbourhoods and wider strategic levels of government more important than in relation to economic policy, especially if the neighbourhood agenda is to close the gap between the most disadvantaged neighbourhoods and the rest of the country. (Taylor and Wilson, 2006, p 7)

The authors draw upon the Joseph Rowntree Foundation's neighbourhoods programme to support their arguments. The programme:

> has highlighted the blocks faced by communities in influencing local power holders. Facilitators employed by the programme to support neighbourhood groups saw it as the main focus of their work – even where they worked on building capacity, power and influence remained the key issue: 'Everything stops at the Town Hall.' (Taylor and Wilson, 2006, p 11)

The potential of the critical community practice model in this kind of situation rests on the unravelling of power and influence, using the different meanings of power to critically appraise the local situation in the wider regional, national and global contexts.

Sharing ideas

The assumption of the critical community practice model is that, while every community is unique, there are common ideas that underpin strategies and actions. The model provides a framework for sharing these ideas. Sometimes this can be achieved through journal articles and conferences. Increasingly, however, it is the internet which enlarges the scope for sharing to take place between projects. Undoubtedly, we shall see more imaginative use of technology by networks of individuals and organisations. The communication of case studies and 'how to do it' practice-theory will be complemented by the exchange of ideas, the explication and adaptation of theories by involved individuals and groups. Globally, this is happening already among civil society organisations where there is an urgency about responding to injustices. It will surely also develop within regeneration and social inclusion programmes in the UK context, perhaps inspired by examples of European networks, which have successfully exchanged good practice not only among activists and practitioners but also researchers and policy makers (for an example of a European Union funded project which achieved this, see Henderson, 2005).

Reforming institutions

This way of applying the critical community practice model places politicians and policy makers themselves in a proactive role. Rather than waiting to respond to the demands of social movements or public opinion they take the initiative to change the ways that institutions and organisations function. The examples given by Hugh Butcher in Chapter Three of neighbourhood governance of schools in Chicago and the participatory budgeting process in Port Alegre illustrate the potential of this idea. It is part of the 'power-with' argument, integrative power that has the capacity to achieve goals with others rather than at the expense of others.

At both national and local levels, a decision to reform institutions will normally require strong leadership from senior politicians. These representatives will have a vision of how changing the structures and organisational procedures of institutions will have long-lasting benefits for the wider community. Parallel to such political leadership there has to be support from, at the government level, senior civil servants, and, at the local authority level, senior officers. This is because the major challenge for institutional reform lies in the implementation phase. This has been evident in the Blair government's attempts to reform local government – strong on promises and rhetoric, weak on producing measurable change. At the same time, most advocates of institutional reform will acknowledge that it is a process that takes time. Organisational and bureaucratic procedures, particularly in large organisations, are so firmly entrenched that changing them requires a combination of patience and persistence.

Concluding comments

The critical community practice model has the potential to be used as a tool for going beyond the idea of dissemination of good practice among professionals. Provided the language used remains accessible the model can be drawn upon by a multiplicity of actors: local activists, practitioners, managers, researchers, commentators, policy makers and politicians. Conceived of in this way, the model can itself contribute to struggles for the increased democratisation of society.

The five suggestions outlined above for how the model can engage with the political and policy dimensions of public life are consistent with our contention that the model should be used as an integrated whole. It is apparent that most of the approaches suggested draw mainly on the community consciousness and community theory components rather than practical critical action. Only in the institutional reform approach does the critical action component of the model come into play in a major way.

The basis of the argument in this chapter is that more attention needs to be given to the power of ideas in the fields to which community practice relates. The process of strengthening communities will not be helped by the combination of pragmatism and funding pressures that has been – and continue to be – so dominant. Our critical community practice model provides a means of countering what is in effect an anti-intellectual tradition in the running of economic and social programmes. That the model is based on the working assumptions and guiding values set out in Chapter Four means that using it to handle and challenge ideas need not end up becoming an elitist exercise, detached from the struggles of communities against social disadvantage and oppression. Engaging with political analysis and dissecting the ideas lying behind government policies is crucial to communities becoming more emancipated, not a luxury.

EIGHT

Becoming critical: developing the community practitioner

Sarah Banks

Introduction

The last three chapters have examined aspects of critical community practice in relation to direct work in and with community groups and organisations (Chapter Five); managing practitioners, programmes and organisations (Chapter Six); and developing policy in the context of the current political climate (Chapter Seven). The focus of attention has been on the processes and activities of groups and organisations and the policy and political context in which the practice takes place. This chapter focuses on the practitioners themselves, in particular on their value commitments and motivations, their capacities for critical reflection and reflexivity and practical wisdom. Our concern in this chapter is with the centre of the diagram given in Chapter Four (Figure 4.1), namely, critical consciousness and value commitments – although as discussed in earlier chapters, all elements are inextricably linked. We first discuss accounts given by practitioners of their orientations to their work, drawing out aspects relevant to critical community practice. We then consider briefly some approaches to supporting and developing the commitment and capacities of critical community practitioners through supervision, dialogue and reflective writing. The accounts from practitioners come mainly from professional workers, with some insights also from policy makers, managers and members of community groups.

Practitioners talking

Although the term 'practice' implies a practitioner, it is often used with a focus on actions and outcomes, rather than the motivations, intentions or purposes of the practitioner. In critical practice the latter are centrally important and inextricably linked with the processes and outcomes of the work. Arguably, in characterising critical community practice, the qualities or dispositions of the practitioner (such as courage or a questioning approach) are just as important as the action taken and outcomes achieved. This chapter draws on several semi-structured interviews with community practitioners who were asked to talk about their motivations for their work, their current dilemmas and challenges. The practitioners interviewed were all engaged in some form of community practice, but were not necessarily selected on the basis that they were thought to exhibit the qualities of the ideal 'critical practitioner'. Indeed, it can be argued that there are degrees of criticality. For example, some practitioners may be very committed to a set of values and able to articulate a coherent and sophisticated political analysis of causes of poverty and oppression, while exhibiting limited capacities for communication, team building and reflection on the nature of their own roles. Alternatively, a group, project or initiative may have emancipatory and empowering aims (such as the schools councils, housing cooperatives or social enterprises discussed in Chapter Three or the asylum seekers' network in Chapter Five), while some of the individual participants might not have very well-developed levels of critical consciousness.

Critical practitioners are always in a state of 'becoming' – developing their awareness, ideas, analysis and capacities through their conversations and actions in collaboration with others. So rather than simply going to projects or initiatives that seem overtly radical in their aims or ethos on the assumption that this is where critical practitioners are to be found, we have engaged in conversations with a range of community practitioners (mainly paid workers, but also some unpaid members of community groups, as well as managers and policy makers) from different types of projects and settings in England. These include: projects in the voluntary sector working with drug users and people with disabilities; local authority youth work, community development and children's services; a local authority cabinet (comprising executive politicians); an asylum seekers' network; and a neighbourhood-based residents' group. The aim is not to be representative of the vast variety of work and types of practitioner that comes under the umbrella of community practice in different regions and countries, but rather to use insights from a range of practitioners to illustrate our discussion. Some of the interviews were conducted specially for this book, while others conducted in connection with related research on the social professions, local authority community development and empowering local communities have also been drawn upon where relevant (see Banks, 2003a; Banks, 2004; Banks and Orton, 2007; Banks and Vickers, 2006).[1]

We have drawn out, from the comments of the interviewees', themes that seem particularly relevant to critical community practice.

Beyond the 'comfort zone'

Building on the discussion in earlier chapters, particularly Chapter Four, one way of encapsulating critical practice is that it is practice that has a critical edge, particularly in terms of a focus on political analysis, the degree of reflexivity of the worker and the level of commitment to values relating to social justice and emancipatory change. Being a critical community practitioner means playing a difficult and often uneasy role. As a local authority youth worker commented: 'I think hitting a comfort zone is just not what you should be able to do in our job.' This was echoed by another practitioner working in a voluntary sector community-based project with adults with drug problems. When asked what motivated her, she commented about the challenging nature of her work:

> It's the relationship I have with the people that I work with. It's not just going into work and knowing exactly how your day's going to pan out, because you don't know how it's going to pan out. You don't know who's going to come in, you don't know what's going to happen. And it is that I do get on well with the people that I work with. And sometimes it's really hard and I think, 'I didn't handle that well, I should do this differently', which is good because *if it was easy and you knew how to do everything I probably wouldn't stay there very long* [emphasis added].

In addition to saying that she feels she has a good relationship with the people using the project, this worker claims that she is motivated by the unpredictability of the work and the fact that she finds it challenging.

There are many other ways that we might describe what is meant by 'critical edge' or 'going beyond the comfort zone'. The youth worker who used the term went on to describe what this meant for her, including 'thinking ahead of the game', and 'reaching for the moment', adding:

> You've got to be a very good reflector, I think, very, very good reflector on yourself and the [youth] centre. You've got

to have a very good overview and not be overcritical. But you've got to be quite critical of what's being provided.

Being a critical practitioner is about more than being a competent and reflective practitioner. It is about being a person of courage, reflexivity and practical wisdom. We may speak of practitioners as 'highly skilled', 'intuitive', 'clever', but what would it take to use the descriptor 'critical practitioner'? Building on the discussions in Chapter Four and drawing on interviews, we first give some examples of what it means to demonstrate commitment, critical consciousness and capacity, before considering how these qualities can be developed in practitioners.

Commitment to a set of values: clarity and strength of belief

We have already identified values centring around social justice as being at the heart of critical community practice. In this context, a value is a belief about what is worthy or valuable. In order for a practitioner to be committed, these values need to be owned, understood and integrated into practice. We would expect a committed practitioner to be able to express their values clearly, explain what they mean and demonstrate them in practice (Banks, 2005). Commitment involves clarity and strength of belief. The youth worker who spoke about moving beyond the comfort zone, spontaneously talked about what she believed in:

> *I really believe in* the group activities ... *I really believe in, for me*, getting them [the young people] out of [name of place] and thinking there's a world a little bit further away ... [emphasis added]

This worker uses the adverb 'really' to add strength to her expression of belief, and repeats the phrase 'I really believe in', which adds further emphasis. She is indicating that she has a purpose in doing the work and she believes in what she is doing. Interestingly, she expresses her values in terms not only of what she does, but what the people she is working with do and think. She does not elaborate, but we might assume she is talking about encouraging the young people themselves to think critically. Another senior youth worker expressed his values in a similar way, but gave more details:

> Challenging things for change, and yes, getting young people to think, and you know, if we could ... headline: 'Youth worker makes young person think' ...Yes, so it's ... *for me*, it's about getting young people to think, about what's going on in their lives, what's going on in their relationships, how they're interacting with each other and the impact that's having on them, you know, and how they can change that, and make life better for them in the future, and others as well. [emphasis added]

Both these workers use the phrase 'for me' – indicating clear ownership of the values they are expressing. The way they describe their values indicates a strength of feeling and genuineness and, in the case of the second worker, an ability to articulate his values, not just in terms of general principles, but what they mean in practice. This kind of clarity and ability to articulate is a prerequisite for expressing value commitments. However, in critical community practice, we need to go a step further and interrogate the content of the values – for example, in the case mentioned above, we would seek to clarify what kind of future is being looked for, or how power is construed in young people's lives.

A manager of an organisation working with people with disabilities described the ability to express values as one of the qualities she looks for when interviewing people who had applied for jobs as support workers for older people and people with disabilities. She explained that she would ask interviewees about their 'value base' in order to assess their suitability for the job. She would ask questions such as: 'What do you believe in?', 'What are the principles you live by?'. She explained that she would expect the interviewees to know what she was talking about and to express values about respecting people and appreciating differences. Some interviewees were not able to do this. She then elaborated, adding more detail about what she appreciates in workers, including passion and evidence of putting values into practice:

> I like it ... when they get a bit *righteously angry* about injustice and stigma, people being disadvantaged, that kind of thing ... I've interviewed people who've talked about respecting people and they come into my team and they don't even treat their colleagues with due respect, and I go: 'Well you don't actually believe that because you don't do it.' But it's very easy to talk about these things. So the people I probably respond to are the ones who seem to

have the *fire in their bellies* and you can spot them, the people
who are passionate about it, but *passion* is quite important I
think. If you're talking about values in a dispassionate way, I
find that quite uncomfortable. If there's no sense of *emotion*
when people are talking about their values I find that very
uncomfortable and unsettling. [emphasis added]

This manager is suggesting that to believe genuinely in a value means
having a strong motivation to put the value into practice. She feels
that a degree of passion is important. This is echoed by the community
activist from the asylum seekers' network discussed in Chapter Five,
who spoke about his motivations for joining the group and taking part
in campaigns as stimulated by anger at the injustices faced by asylum
seekers in Britain. As Leonard (1997, p 162) comments, in the context
of his arguments for the reconstruction of emancipatory practice: 'Anger
is the human attribute which has the most possibility of generating
the kind of individual and collective resistance which is a necessary
precondition of emancipation.'

Passion may, indeed, be one sign of commitment, and many
practitioners do use the language of emotion to describe themselves
and their work (see, for example, the study of regeneration workers
by Hoggett et al, 2006). Another of our interviewees, a local authority
community development worker, spoke about being 'driven' and about
'passion' when asked how he became involved in community work:

I'm really *driven* by stuff around equal opportunities. I'm
quite *passionate* about that as well and *I believe in* working
with people from the bottom up and supporting them in
the process of challenging and promoting change at a local
level. [emphasis added]

This worker kept coming back to passion in his interview:

I'm quite a *strong* person, sort of *deep down* I'm quite
passionate about my beliefs and when I do something I'll
jump over every sort of mountain and *strive* to do it and get
there and that *drive* and *passion* within me is really important.
If I'm really doing something and I'm involved in it and
enjoying it I'll put the *energy* I've got into it, but obviously
it needs to be focused and not fragmented and it needs to

be joined up with what other people do, so you need a consistent approach across the area. [emphasis added]

Here the community development worker is describing passion as important, but stressing that it needs to be balanced by consistency (implying, perhaps, some strategic thinking).

However, there may be other practitioners who demonstrate consistency, clarity and strength of purpose in their practice, whom we might not describe as 'passionate'. The regeneration manager, who was in overall charge of the neighbourhood regeneration programme discussed in Chapter Five, and in Banks (2003a), spoke of how she approached her work with local residents:

> I think it goes back to some basic principles really, which is as far as we can, you know ... we do try to be as open and inclusive as possible ... My experience is that if you mean it and you show that you mean it and you demonstrate that, then you can pull up a lot of trust.

She spoke about 'being consistent', about giving people feedback after a meeting, letting people know what is happening, adding:

> I think that's an important principle really. If you involve people in whatever, agencies or residents in planning or decision making, they won't all be involved in the delivery but you need to let them know what's happening.

This manager was able both to articulate a working principle and to show how she put it into practice. She explained that 'it's not just what I think' and that the approach was beginning to be reflected in statements of purpose and philosophy for the programme that all the partner agencies and residents sign up to, and 'we actually try and stick to it'. She gave an example relating to:

> The kind of things which I thought were fairly small and trivial and unimportant but residents thought were quite important. Like, for example, if they're involved in a meeting and somebody is taking the minutes, they actually want the minutes within a week. They want to know. They want a reference point, and they want to be able to remember. They want a record of what was said and done, and they want it in there and they can use it to come back and say:

'You said this, we agreed that.' And I'd never really thought about anything like that. I never would have thought they would want the minutes of stuff, but they do.

This worker's values of openness and inclusivity have led her to listen hard and respect what local residents, her partners in the regeneration programme, say they want in order to feel included. In reflecting on this, she expresses surprise and begins to locate herself in the picture, which leads us to the next feature of the critical practitioner, which is also intimately linked with value commitments, namely, critical consciousness.

Critical self-awareness and reflexivity

Critical consciousness involves practitioners being aware of themselves, their own values, the values of the agency for which they work, the political context of the work and the influence these have on the work that they do. As discussed in Chapter Four, a key component of critical consciousness is reflexivity. The term 'reflexivity' is used in several ways by different theorists, and sometimes interchangeably with 'reflection'. However, 'reflexivity' is often used to mean a kind of 'critical reflection'. If reflection is about practitioners examining what happened or is happening in a piece of practice, considering why and where to go next, then reflexivity adds a further dimension of 'locating our own perspective in the discourse' (Fook, 2002, p 92). Fook distinguishes reflective processes from a reflexive stance, arguing that the former are underpinned by the latter. Bolton (2005, p 10) has a useful description of reflexivity as:

> Making aspects of the self strange; focusing close attention upon *one's own* actions, thoughts, feelings, values, identity and their effect upon others, situations, and professional and social structures.

Reflexivity has been described by various authors as being about questioning, examining and becoming aware of personal assumptions and values, dominant professional constructions influencing practice and other taken-for-granted assumptions (Brechin, 2000; Taylor and White, 2000). Bourdieu (1992) speaks of uncovering the 'unthought categories' which themselves are preconditions of our more self-conscious practices. Lash (1994, p 155) interprets these unthought categories as 'predispositions and orientations' – our own habits.

Seeing this in terms of our model of critical community practice (Figure 4.1), we can also locate the link with critical theorising, which helps us to place our own values, orientations and assumptions in their sociopolitical context.

Reflexivity can often be encouraged through the practitioners writing journals or diaries about practice or describing and analysing critical incidents. A community and youth work student who was undertaking a period of fieldwork practice in a project for people with disabilities brought in to the university a written account of a piece of practice which raised ethical issues for her. In her account she explained that she was undertaking a placement at a disability initiative run by an independent local voluntary organisation established by and for people with disabilities. The people using the project mainly had physical disabilities, but some people had mental health issues and learning difficulties. The student described how on her first day she spent some time talking to an older man, Paul, with slight mobility problems, who 'spent his time making tea and going to the toilet'. She commented: 'I presumed he had slight learning difficulties as he does not communicate with others a great deal and simply appears unmotivated.' She later discovered from a member of staff that he had previously managed a shop and was suffering from a degenerative physical condition. She commented: 'I now view Paul in a different light, which I know is wrong. Consequently this has made me reconsider the way I approach and interact with each member of the centre.' She explained this further:

> Since leaving school I have spent approximately 10 years working with people with special needs, including learning difficulties, behavioural problems and physical disabilities. So maybe my mindset is at fault here and I need to consider what is going on in the present.

In presenting her case to the student group, she commented about her thoughts and actions and raised questions about how to approach such work in the future. These included:

> I thought: 'This isn't right'...

> With all my experience, I still went in there prejudging.

She framed the second part of her written account (the analysis) as an ethical dilemma centred around the question of whether she should read the personal records of the users of the project or ask staff questions about each member: 'Do I need to know people's medical history to know how to interact with them?' She felt she did not know the answer to this question, so took it to her supervision session with the deputy manager. Her supervisor explained that the project did not keep details of medical history, as this was not felt to be important and staff should get to know users on their own terms. This sparked further reflection and debate in the student's learning journal.

The example above from the community and youth work student shows how something unexpected or surprising sparks a revisiting of the worker's attitudes, values and approach to an area of work in which she had a long experience.

Another of the voluntary sector practitioners interviewed had worked abroad on two occasions, in Japan and the Pacific Islands, and commented on how this provoked her to re-evaluate who she was and how she did things:

> You definitely do get to know yourself better because people will ask you questions abroad that they would never ask you here, because it's kind of unwritten, understood why things are done this way. Whereas in another culture it doesn't make any sense, so you kind of begin to think: 'Oh, OK, there is a different way to do it.' And then you begin to think: 'Why did I do it this way?', and think more about kind of why you think the way you think – because you kind of have to start explaining it to other people.

Similar types of challenges were reported by community activists in the asylum seekers' network, when the diverse cultural backgrounds and faith commitments of asylum-seeker members caused UK group members to see their own political commitments and tactics in a new light. At the opposite end of the spectrum, politicians in local government reported on the impact of undertaking a programme of training in community development with fellow councillors and a range of local government employees from different sections of the council, commenting that it 'raised awareness' and 'offered a new perspective'. One senior policy-making councillor reflected that as a result of the training, based on the use of a model of community development with empowering values at its heart: 'I looked at what I'd done previously and consciously checked it against the model.' This was part of a process of developing awareness and critical consciousness among policy makers.

Capacity to put values into practice: practical wisdom and praxis

Most of the descriptions given above of practitioners' own accounts of their value commitments and their consciousness of themselves and their values have also included accounts of them putting their values into practice. It would hardly make sense to say that someone was committed to a set of values linked to social justice and emancipatory change if they did not exemplify these values in their actions. If they did not, then we might describe them as disingenuous, in bad faith or exhibiting weakness of will. However, it is certainly true to say that some people may be more skilful or adept in living out their values than others. A practitioner may have a passionate commitment to work for social justice, yet may end up alienating people, rushing into action without thinking, misjudging timing, personalities or strategies. Many theorists of professional practice refer to Aristotle's concept of *phronesis* or practical wisdom as a key ingredient in skilful practice. This is not the same as logic or rationality – rather it is an ability to make discerning judgements, based on sensitivity, perceptiveness and practical reasoning. According to Frank (2004, p 221), phronesis is 'the opposite of acting on the basis of scripts and protocols', that is, it involves creativity, flexibility and attention to context.

Smith (1994, p 76), in his study of informal and community educators (youth, community and adult education workers), uses the Aristotelian concept of practical wisdom, describing it as 'a disposition to act truly and justly', entailing an orientation to 'good' or 'right' rather than correct action. He uses this to develop a 'praxis model' of local education practice, which he describes as driven by general principles, being explicit about the interests it serves and making an explicit commitment to emancipation. He describes praxis as informed, committed action. Others have described it as a synthesis of reflection and action or theory and action (Freire, 1972; Ledwith, 2005). Smith's use of the term 'committed', however, emphasises the integration of values into the action. On this reading, 'praxis' can be thought of as putting values into practice on the basis of practical wisdom.

The voluntary sector drugs worker mentioned earlier, when asked what her core values were, began her reply with the following statement: 'Instilling the equality and challenging what I see to be inequality are two values that I work towards.' For her, 'equality' clearly entailed working with the people using the project in a way that promoted their capacity for self-determination. She elaborated on this as follows:

> Sometimes I have more issues with how other staff are with the clients. Like some staff have had a homeless client, they've taken their washing home and done their washing. Some staff have brought in clothes or shoes, whatever, that they might have had left over from their children ... People are kind of mothering the clients in a way and that doesn't sit quite right with me. But then again you feel awful because you might have something spare that somebody needs.

She gave an example of a service user who had no cooking facilities to whom she passed on a leaflet about a cheap cooking stove: 'I know he's got some money and this is really cheap. That's the sort of way I would go about it, rather than saying: "here you go".' Clearly, this practitioner was translating her value of 'equality' into practice as promoting people's capacities to make their own choices and take action themselves. In the longer term, this would be one stage in a process whereby they might eventually be in a position to play a role in participatory democratic governance (see Chapter Three) in the homelessness project or in wider society.

The challenge of how to put values into practice is often quite prominent for community practitioners. A local authority community development worker described how the community development team in which she worked had developed a 'community engagement toolkit' alongside a training programme for use by councillors and officers wishing to undertake community consultations and work more participatively with local communities. While this was felt to be a positive development, encouraging better consultation and participation processes, there was also a fear that community development values would be diluted or forgotten as 'community engagement' becomes a management objective. Promoting 'community engagement' in a mechanistic fashion, perhaps setting up opportunities for consultation with local people over certain issues, may be far removed from critical community practice. However, in this community development team it was recognised that the work they do is often a compromise between pragmatism about what is achievable and idealism about staying true to their values. They may feel somewhat uncomfortable and as if they are 'selling out'.

The term 'toolkit' has connotations of accessibility and usefulness, but it also implies that it can be picked up by anyone with a modicum of skill in the use of the tools, taken out, used and put back in a cupboard. To promote a toolkit for this work has some danger of reducing the process to a set of discrete skills. Yet if a toolkit encourages more awareness of how to consult local communities in ways that are open, fair and clear, then this could be thought of as a positive development. Preparing and promoting the toolkit could be regarded as a step along the road towards the longer-term goals of promoting more democratic and empowering local governance. As one of the other members of the community development team commented:

> What makes me tick is the social justice agenda. I do try and do my best for people, but I'll compromise, duck and dive … It's like a game of football.

All members of this team were very aware of the constraints of working as community development workers in a local authority, but felt it was, nevertheless, worthwhile, as they were able to stimulate changes in how the council worked. Another team member described the situation as follows:

> In this work, you pick people to work with that you know you can get on with. You wouldn't normally pick [name of local authority]. We have to accept that we work for a council, with all the pressures that brings. We rail against things we have no control over. But really we should see opportunities.

As one of his colleagues commented: 'You still carry the values with you, but you have cleverer ways of going about it [putting them into practice].' What gives this practice its critical edge are the intentions and strategic direction of the practitioners.

Developing the critical community practitioner

We have spent some time unpicking what might be entailed in being a committed and reflexive critical practitioner, drawing on accounts given by a range of community practitioners of their day-to-day practice. We now consider briefly a range of ways of developing and supporting the critical practitioner.

There is no single recipe for developing the qualities of the critical practitioner, but several sources of stimulation and encouragement can be identified, all of which are underpinned by the notion that there is a community of practitioners who are a source of stimulation, debate and values clarification. Activities and processes include education and training, supervision, mentoring, peer debate and support, reflective writing, reading and practitioner research. All of these would be considered a normal part of professional development – it is the way they are approached that makes them distinctive in relation to critical practice. We would expect a dynamic and challenging learning relationship between tutor and student, supervisor and supervisee, colleague and colleague, writer and writing, reader and text, practitioner researcher and people and issues researched. This might involve working with the practitioner in the process of:

- clarifying and questioning personal, professional, organisational and political values;
- identifying underlying assumptions or dominant narratives in the discourses of practitioners and others;
- challenging dominant discourses that are disempowering;
- being honest about the power relations in situations, while working towards greater equality;
- paying attention to the whole context in which the practice takes place.

Much of the literature on reflective practice and critical thinking suggests approaches that can be used in education and training for practitioners in the welfare, health, caring and community field (Bolton, 2005; Brechin et al, 2000; Fook, 2002; Schön, 1987, 1991; Wilson and Wilde, 2001). In this chapter we focus on three approaches to practitioner development that may be less well developed, particularly in relation to community practice, namely: critical supervision; practitioner dialogue and debate; and reflective writing. We will not elaborate on the 'technical' or practical capacities and skills needed for critical community practice because, as indicated earlier, there is no recipe that can be followed. Rather, what is important is the repertoire that can be drawn upon by practitioners using their creative and critical abilities. Details of basic skills can be found in manuals and textbooks about community work, community organising and transformatory practice (see, for example, Association of Community Workers, 2001; Hardcastle et al, 2004; Henderson and Thomas, 2002; Hope and Timmel, 1999). The important issue for critical community practice is how to deploy them with critical awareness.

Critical supervision

Supervision as a focus for practitioner support and development is well established in social work and related fields such as counselling (Brown and Bourne, 1996; Lawton and Felton, 2000), but less so in many other areas of work that involve community practitioners. Even in social work, where it is an accepted part of professional practice, supervision may be very task-focused and managerial, paying little attention to professional education and development. With its connotations of hierarchy, oversight and control, supervision may not seem like a very fruitful arena for critical practice development. However, the supervisory relationship can have many forms other than the one-to-one oversight of a practitioner by a manager. Supervision can be conducted in groups, by peers or by non-managerial consultants. Its focus may be managerial, but it is commonly recognised as having two other functions, namely education and support (Hawkins and Shohet, 2000).

The potential for critical supervision with a focus on learning can be seen very clearly in the student–supervisor relationship, where the 'supervisor' may actually be designated by a title such as 'practice teacher' or 'fieldwork tutor'. The tone for the supervisory relationship can be set by the terms of reference drawn up at the start, which may lay out the expectations of all parties, the kinds of agenda items that would be expected or materials that should be brought. A student undertaking a professional education programme, such as the community and youth work student in the disability project mentioned earlier, may be invited to come to the supervision session prepared with extracts from a reflective diary, notes of critical incidents or accounts of ethical dilemmas. Students new to an agency or a particular role may experience puzzlement and confusion, and may begin to question their assumptions, prejudices and values, as did the community and youth work student we quoted earlier. If they do not, then the good practice teacher will see it as part of her role to challenge and question student practitioners by:

- asking for accounts of practice that fully contextualise significant pieces of work, events, situations or relationships (identifying all the actors involved and lines of power, for example);
- encouraging them to locate themselves in the context and the action taking place, identifying their own influence and power;
- encouraging them to identify their own values and motivations;
- linking analysis of practice to relevant theories and concepts.

This approach to supervision, while recognised as part of the student learning experience, often disappears for qualified practitioners, who sometimes have no supervision at all, or else experience a much more managerial, task-focused supervisory relationship. Phillipson (2002, p 250), discussing the limitations of much supervision in social work, asks the question: 'What might it be like to have "emancipatory practice" as an agenda item?'. While it would probably be unnecessary, or too intense, to engage regularly in the kind of critical, challenging supervisions that are offered by the best student supervisors, periodic critical reflection and reflexivity undertaken in the company of one or more supportive colleagues can help maintain a critical edge to the work. A critical friend – a colleague or a peer – can provide stimulation, or a team or group supervision session may offer the opportunity for a wide range of perspectives on a particular issue or problem (Proctor, 2000).

Practitioner dialogue and debate

The concept of critical practice is underpinned by the idea of a community of practitioners. The opportunity to discuss, debate and agonise with colleagues is a vital part of keeping critical practice alive and the critical practitioner motivated and supported. A team of like-minded people is, of course, the ideal setting. The community development team mentioned earlier is a good example – a small group of practitioners, all employed as community development officers, based in the same office, working in the context of a large, diverse local authority. While each practitioner has a different background, different strengths, skills and predilections, they all share a common professional discourse of community development work. When one of the authors of this book was a participant-observer in several team meetings (albeit, set up explicitly to reflect on the work of the team), it was clear that the team members were critically conscious of the precariousness of their role in a large local authority, the challenges to the shared values of community development work, and would discuss and debate these issues together.

Multi-professional and inter-professional teams have to work harder to engage in dialogue, but if achieved, they can provide even more challenging and provocative settings for developing critical practice. Accepted professional values and ways of doing things can be questioned. A qualified nurse, working in a community-based setting as part of a youth offending team, for example, found his values and practices, in relation to professional–service user confidentiality, were questioned in the context of whole-team working (Banks, 2004, pp 142–3).

Often, team or staff meetings, rather like supervision sessions, if they happen at all, are focused on information sharing, strategic developments and immediate tasks. However, time can be set aside for critical reflection on the work of the team or on individuals' issues. Alternatively, a special forum can be established. For example, a senior social worker working on a Sure Start programme (multi-agency working with children and parents) reported having set up a 'reflective practice forum' that meets once a fortnight. She commented that three counsellors had joined the group, which was proving helpful and challenging, as they were bringing new perspectives. She commented: 'I genuinely learn something every time we meet.'

Seminars, action-learning sets and reading groups are all ways of offering mutual support and constructive challenge. For community practitioners who are members and activists in self-managed groups, education and training, or focused discussions around a specific theme or issue, provide similar opportunities (as exemplified in Chapter Five in the learning programme undertaken by members of the community action partnership and the focus group discussion for asylum seekers). For managers, especially senior managers, it may be quite difficult to sustain a critical approach in an organisational climate of performance management, working to externally defined targets and financial challenges. Informal networks of people in senior positions, which focus not just on support, but also critical dialogue, debate and a questioning of the current policy context, can prove a useful forum for practitioner development – for example learning circles, lunches or action learning sets.

Reflective writing

Practitioners in training are often asked to keep a reflective diary or learning journal, especially during the fieldwork practice period (Banks, 2003b). For many, despite the fact that they comment on how useful they find the exercise, this may be the only time they undertake such reflective writing about their work. Reflective writing, whether in journal or other format, structured or a stream of consciousness, prose or verse, fact or fiction, shared or kept private, can be a very useful tool for encouraging both reflection and critical reflection or reflexivity. It may also include drawings or diagrams (such as mind maps) to help make sense of the work, tease out assumptions, issues and examine goals and ways forward. Bolton (2005) offers a very useful overview of a whole range of possibilities for using and encouraging reflective writing in the context of professional development, including stories, use of metaphor and poetry, learning journals and facilitation of writing groups. Some guidance or training in reflective writing is important, otherwise, as Trotter (1999, quoted in Bolton, 2005, p 172) notes in the context of learning journals, entries may tend to be 'observational and reactionary rather than reflective'.

Hatton and Smith (1995) offer a framework for recognising 'reflectivity' in writing as follows (quoted in Moon, 1999, p 103):

1. *Descriptive writing* – a description of events or literature reports. No discussion beyond description.
2. *Descriptive reflection* – description of events, plus some justification in relatively descriptive language. The possibility of alternative viewpoints in discussion is accepted. Reflection may be based generally on one perspective or factor as rationale or, presumably in a more sophisticated form, is based on the recognition of multiple factors and perspectives.
3. *Dialogic reflection* – demonstrates a stepping back from the events and actions leading to a different level of mulling about discourse with self and exploring the discourse of events and actions. The reflection is analytical or integrative, linking factors and perspectives. It may reveal inconsistency in attempting to provide rationales and critiques.
4. *Critical reflection* – demonstrates an awareness that actions and events are not only located within and explicable by multiple perspectives, but are located in and influenced by multiple historical, ethical and sociopolitical contexts.

A facilitator of reflective writing may have to work with practitioners to develop skills first in good description, before then moving on to encourage a critical reflective approach, which may be stimulated by asking participants to undertake specific writing tasks. There follows an example of a structured piece of writing relating to ethical issues in practice requested as part of a learning journal – but equally appropriate for use in a workshop or supervision session (adapted from Banks, 2003b):

> Think of an event or situation that raised/is raising ethical issues for you. This might be a situation you found/are finding problematic, conflictual, and/or where it was/is

difficult to make a decision. Issues of rights, duties, human welfare, fairness, justice or equality may be involved.

1. *Briefly describe what happened* (the key events, people, circumstances).
2. *Identify the ethical issues involved* and comment on them (for example: people's rights to space and freedom from harassment; equality of opportunity; fairness in the use of resources; professional duties and responsibilities).
3. *Contextualise your account* in relation to broader geographical, policy, theory and practice considerations (for example, area-based policies for tackling multiple deprivation, local power structures and networks, dominant economic discourses).
4. *Reflections*:
   - Reflect on what action was taken and/or could have been taken. Why was it taken? What could have been done differently? Locate the action in terms of the relevant contextual factors.
   - Reflect on your role (including your own power/lack of power) and your emotions.
   - Reflect on what you have learnt from analysing and reflecting on this situation/event.
   - What further action do you need to take in relation to this situation or similar ones in the future?

Conclusions

This chapter has continued the work of elaborating the nature of critical community practice, in this case through analysing some of the voices of practitioners. We have looked in a bit more depth at what it means for practitioners to exhibit commitment to a set of values centring on social justice, to exhibit critical awareness of their roles and to use practical wisdom in their actions and decision making.

As earlier chapters have shown, the role of the critical community practitioner is complex and challenging. There are no set recipes that can be used by practitioners themselves, or by their mentors, managers and teachers, to develop their critical consciousness, capacity and commitment. However, the role of dialogue with oneself and colleagues, a questioning of experience, and the reinforcement and development of values and commitment within a community of critical practitioners is vitally important. We hope that reading articles, accounts of practice and books like this can also play a part in stimulating, reinforcing and clarifying ideas and prompting further discussion with colleagues and other key actors in the field of community practice.

Note

[1] We are grateful to those practitioners whose interviews with Sarah Banks are used in this chapter, and to Cynthia Bisman of Bryn Mawr College, USA, for allowing us to draw on some interviews she undertook in the UK in 2006. All interviewees and places have been anonymised.

NINE

Conclusions

Paul Henderson

Introduction

In the preceding chapters we have drawn on a wide range of case studies and examples. We have referred also, in the UK context, to a variety of groups, professions and jobs. If this is circumstantial evidence that community practice has expanded and become more generic, the substantive evidence for making this claim rests on the extent to which 'community' and community involvement have become part of the mainstream of government policy making. The emphasis given by the government to the need for partnership working, and its more tentative commitment to developing the idea of governance at the local level, are the main concrete manifestations of this policy. Community practice, encouraged and driven by community policies, is widespread. It is also in need of more analysis and support.

The advancement by the authors of the idea of *critical* community practice has resulted in a publication which, compared with the two earlier books on community practice, is lodged more obviously within theory rather than practice or policy. Essentially, this volume is offering a theoretical underpinning for community practice which, as emphasised throughout the book, needs to have an explicit critical edge. A significant implication of this approach is that each writer adopts a slightly different perspective on critical community practice. This reflects, on the one hand, the different ways in which theory is used and articulated and, on the other, varying interpretations placed on the concept of critical community practice.

On the first point, some people will use theory as a 'light touch', seeing it as essentially informing actions and decisions rather than determining them. Others, however, draw upon theory in a much more direct way, thereby giving it a more powerful imprint on actions and decisions. The second point demonstrates the importance of interpreting a difficult concept such as critical community practice. It is not set in stone. Just as the movement of a symphony can be played in contrasting ways under different conductors, so the idea of critical community practice – and how it is applied in myriad practice and policy settings – can be given different emphases. Thus we offer an explanation, but no apology or excuse, for the different 'takes' on critical community practice that readers will have noted.

The value of critical community practice

We anticipate the concept of critical community practice being subjected to a variety of levels and forms of analysis and interpretation. Do the arguments stand up? Are the examples and case studies provided relevant to the concept? These and other questions will, we hope, probe the value of the concept. At this point, however, we wish to ask three practical questions concerning its value: is the concept useful in terms of its applicability? What are the resource implications? Can the model be transferred to settings outside the UK?

On the first question we are in no doubt. This can be illustrated by an example taken from an action-research project on rural community development being run under the auspices of the Carnegie UK Trust's Commission on Rural Community Development. In 2006, organisations in England, Scotland, Wales, Northern Ireland and the Republic of Ireland organised focus groups to collect information and ideas on the current and future skills needed for there to be effective rural community development. In England the focus groups were run by staff from ACRE (Action with Communities in Rural England) and the University of Gloucestershire. Separate meetings were held for community activists, community workers, community work managers/ planners and related professionals (there was also one joint meeting of representatives from each of these groups). Here we see in action the potential relevance of the critical community practice model to key target groups. If we look more closely at the membership of the related professionals group – because of its central importance in the definition of community practice – this gives an insight into the kind of staff who can make use of the model. This particular focus group was attended by a planning consultant, a sustainable development officer, a district council re-housing manager, an academic, planning officers from two district councils, a borough council rural housing enabler and a city council economic development manager.

It is in instances such as this that the critical community practice model can be used – either at the time, or in reflection later – across the spheres of practice, management and policy. The 'community turn' referred to in Chapter Seven, and the advance of a managerialist 'turn' that includes a significant community component, means that a range of actors in these spheres will find that the model relates strongly to them, and can be picked up, interpreted and used by them. The evidence is that this pool of actors will continue to expand.

A major resource implication of using the model will be organisational. In particular, senior managers and policy makers will have to find additional resources to enable staff and others to study and engage with the ideas in the model and their practical implications. The training plans and budgets of organisations will, therefore, need to be worked on.

Perhaps the more interesting resource implication, however, can be drawn from the model itself, in particular its insistence on the importance of the model's values and theoretical assumptions being of paramount importance. This means that organisations and groups are required to support a values-driven practice, resulting in practitioners and managers having the latitude to go outside a strictly target-driven approach. An example would be where a community group or a network of practitioners identified specific learning needs that had not been planned for originally. New resources would have to be found to enable those needs to be met – only then would practice be driven by values. Given the pressures on all of those involved in critical community practice, and expectations that they will keep to established targets and outputs, this kind of resource implication will undoubtedly present a challenge.

We can be more confident when considering the question of the model's transferability. Similar trends to those taking place in the UK can be observed in other countries. However, it is the strength and relevance of the arguments and ideas contained in the model on which its transferability will turn. We believe the model will be of interest to any society that affirms its commitment to democracy and civil society and which acts on such a commitment. Recognition of the legitimacy and role of a not-for-profit sector, and guaranteeing the freedom of its members and supporters to engage in debate and campaigning, will also be required.

Two other points are worth noting. The first is the growing significance of networks of practitioners and others sharing their knowledge, skills and opinions through the use of new technology. Social movements have shown how this can be done globally and others are following suit. Issues surrounding critical community practice could form part of this kind of exchange. The second is to recall that the concept of critical community practice has important theoretical and practice connections with related disciplines and professions: critical social work practice, critical youth work practice, critical regeneration practice, etc. This means that the entry point for critical community practice in other societies is broad. In some countries it could be through social work institutions and networks that the concept is discussed, in others it could be via social enterprise, regeneration or planning: the concept of critical practice is understood in these various fields and this is likely to facilitate connections being made with critical community practice.

Critiquing the model

In several chapters we have emphasised the need for the critical community practice model to be adapted and interpreted. The model draws upon concepts which are deeply contestable and it would be surprising if it did not provoke discussion and debate – criticism in the fullest sense of that term. Furthermore, the model exists within a political, economic and social context and, because this is constantly changing, the model will not stand still. It is in this spirit that we offer our critical thoughts on the model, points where an argument may be weak, where an assumption may be questionable or where we assess that the model needs further study and development.

- *Given the contemporary context, does the emphasis given to the importance of values reflect naivety on our part?* We are referring to the context of target and output-driven programmes and the attention given, in the public, private and voluntary sectors, to efficiency and effectiveness. Yet while values may no longer be prominent in public discourse, they have not disappeared entirely. They may not receive a hearing when plans for expanding gambling or extending the licensing laws are announced but they will often come to the surface when, for example, a particularly violent crime has been committed. One senses that citizens in general are prepared to allow society to change – accepting that some people have become more violent, materialistic, individualistic, avaricious, and so on – but only up to a certain point. It is as if a line can be drawn in the sand: so far and no further. If one then adds in the campaigning work of individuals and organisations who do take a value-based stance on issues, an over-pessimistic view that says that values are disappearing from our lives can be seen to lack validity. Indeed, the range of values-based issues to which people are committed is remarkable. Some of these come within the tradition of charitable giving, others within that of campaigning. Both have global dimensions.

What we can draw from this is that the case for a values-based critical community practice has to be made, and made again. Thus, while the emphasis on values in the model may be over-optimistic about the constancy and profile of values in the public domain, the criticism that the centrality of values in the model is naive is, we contend, misplaced.

- *Is the model over-theoretical?* Hugh Butcher states at the beginning of Chapter Four that a set of theoretical assumptions lies at the heart of the model. Furthermore, the book as a whole is making the case for the power and influence of ideas to be taken more seriously by advocates and practitioners of 'community' and community involvement. Many of the pronouncements on these issues have been alarmingly atheoretical. If this means that the model we put forward is over-theoretical, perhaps we should plead guilty: we have sought to provide an antidote to the flurry of activities – consultation papers, initiatives, programmes – that community activists, practitioners and managers are expected to act upon. The risk is that these actors are pushed to implement the activities without being given the thinking and reflecting time to consider them properly.

  The criticism, however, that the model is over-theoretical may need to be answered in a different way. Ultimately, the question will depend upon the model's relevance and usefulness. We have sought to communicate this by including case studies and examples and by suggesting ways in which the model can be applied in the policy and political context (Chapter Seven) and used in supervision, practitioner dialogue and reflective writing (Chapter Eight). If these and other ways of using the model are shown to work, then the charge that the model is over-theoretical falls by the wayside. Ideas, many of them difficult and contestable, can inform and guide the realities of critical community practice. The jury on this particular charge must, accordingly, remain out for the time being.

- *Is the model over-optimistic about civil society?* With this criticism much depends on how one conceives civil society relating to and working with state institutions. Commenting on his appointment as chair of the Carnegie Inquiry on the Future of Civil Society, Geoff Mulgan stated:

  > At its best civil society is where people express their most important passions and commitments. It is where they challenge power. And it is where they shape the future by responding to new needs and innovating new solutions. The job of the Carnegie Commission will be to look at how best

> to ensure its future health, and how to ensure that it remains robustly independent. (Carnegie UK Trust, 2006, p 2)

This is satisfactory as far as it goes. The key question is how civil society organisations can carry through their commitments. Is it always from a position of contestation with the state? Or, as suggested in this volume, is it also by working in concert with state institutions? We make the case that it is through the second of these two options that progress can be made. Given that as a basis, the criticism that the model is over-optimistic about civil society can be refuted. The scope for civil society organisations that take a multi-faceted strategic approach to informing, campaigning and lobbying is considerable whereas if those organisations adopt a strategy that does not allow for joint working with state bodies, the scope will be limited: civil society organisations would run the risk of boxing themselves in, of playing a limited role in society. It is only on that basis that the argument holds up that the critical community practice model is over-optimistic about civil society.

• *Is the model under-developed?* Our response to this criticism is clear: undoubtedly the model is under-developed. It needs to be 'filled out', not only in the context of the UK but also that of the rest of Europe and other regions of the world. It would be fascinating, for example, to have a critique of the model given from the perspective of Holland, a country that has a history of community development and urban regeneration almost as long as the UK. It also has a tradition of engaging with new ideas, and of sharing them, as well as testing their applicability in practice. It is such a 'mix' of theory and practice, reflecting diverse cultures, that is needed.

There is also a case for undertaking action research in order to expose the model to investigation. This could be done at a number of different levels, from the micro-context of the neighbourhood, to partnership working across a local authority area to the level of national policy making. Such an investment would ensure that analysis and discussion of the model developed a dynamic which could be sustained over the long term. More importantly, it would mean that the plethora of regeneration, social inclusion, health improvement and other programmes that are required by the government to have a significant commitment to community involvement could be scrutinised and debated through the framework of the critical community practice model.

Ideas, policy and practice

Underlying the preceding chapters is a concern that, in the context of critical community practice, a more equitable relationship between ideas, policy and practice can be achieved. At present, it is the first of these which is weak. Policy formulation is strong. Practice, however, suffers from neglect: it is not being challenged and supported adequately by theory and it is being pressurised by the demands of policy. The case for bringing theory back into fashion is a strong one, provided it is accessible and relevant to practice and policy.

Our discussion of critical community practice points to the major shift that is taking place in the relationship between government and communities. On the whole, the shift is to be welcomed. Despite the inherent difficulty of defining 'community', all of us are aware that it remains fundamental to any well-functioning, democratic society. The resourcefulness and networks that exist in communities are constantly being rediscovered. Supporting grass-roots action and engaging with communities on a partnership basis is thus vitally important. Such recognition must, however, be accompanied by analysis of what the 'community' and community involvement dimensions of policy mean for the various key actors involved:

- *Local people:* How do they experience the community involvement imperative? And which local people? Are the policies, for example, too gender-blind, ignoring the situation of many women? To what extent do the policies seek to reach the concerns and priorities of young people? A key issue in all these questions is to ensure that local people receive the kind of recognition, support and resources they are looking for – so that the policies make sense to them.
- *Communities of interest and identity:* Do community involvement and engagement policies relate to these kinds of communities effectively? This question is of vital importance in the context of community cohesion and networks:

> Networks can help to anticipate and diffuse tensions before they become full conflicts. By tackling ignorance, dogma and prejudice, a foundation of understanding and empathy can be established for analysing and dealing with differences … Cross-cutting area-based forums provide opportunities to build bridging and linking social capital, creating relationships between people from different backgrounds and with different remits. (Gilchrist, 2004, p 54)

We can see here the significance of networks both for the interest and identity groups themselves and for bringing different groups into dialogue with each other. Alison Gilchrist emphasises, however, that in the latter situation, inequalities in power and access must be addressed as otherwise there is a risk of re-enforcing the disempowerment of community members, especially those from already marginalised groups.

- *Professional practitioners:* The key point about this group is the need for policy makers and others to realise the range of practitioners whose roles and tasks relate to critical community practice. This includes not only staff such as regeneration officers, whose work in and with communities derives from community involvement policies, but also those practitioners whose work, sometimes implicitly rather than explicitly, brings them into more intermittent contact with communities, for example economic development staff, planning officers, health visitors and housing officers. It is these kinds of practitioners who constitute a key resource for communities. However, the potential of this has, in many instances, still to be realised.

- *Managers:* One of the main implications for the manager's role drawn by Smalle and Henderson (2003) from their case studies in *Managing community practice* is that managers who are responsible for regeneration and social inclusion programmes not only need to be aware of the nature and extent of the problems facing many communities but also need to play an active part in helping to deal with and resolve problems. It is this point that is of similar importance in critical community practice: managers who provide high quality support and supervision for practitioners but who also engage with communities themselves. If such a way of working is to gather pace, there are training and capacity-building implications for managers which the local authority associations and training bodies need to address.

- *Politicians and policy makers:* At different points in the book we have argued for the relevance of critical community practice to politicians and policy makers. The make-up or membership of both groups needs to be specified. When this is done the scope for the groups to engage with critical community practice becomes more evident: for example, a senior elected member of a local authority who has responsibility for housing can connect with the community dimensions of housing officers' work, not only their housing responsibilities.

An important aspect of this volume is for critical community practice to throw light on how the above 'players' can engage with the significant changes taking place in the relationship between government and communities. It will, we believe, help to explain the changes and to place them within a broader context, one that embraces both the politics of change and the theoretical assumptions. To engage seriously with this context it is essential for those involved in critical community practice to be open to new ideas and to commit themselves to exploring them. This requires them to connect their local and national experiences, and reflection, to a global framework of ideas.

The themes and theories contained within the concept of critical community practice are not simply matters for armchair discussion. The place of 'community' in society, and the ways in which citizens, professional practitioners, managers and policy makers can improve dialogue and cooperation between communities and the state, should not be conceived as taking place on the margins of politics and policy making. The fragmentation of some communities and the sense of distance between them and state institutions are major challenges. So too is the search by individuals for ways of acquiring a more meaningful sense of community. If these issues are not addressed then the fragility of representative and participatory democracy, to which we have drawn attention, will be threatened. Our contention, accordingly, is that critical community practice needs to move more to centre stage – urgently.

References

Abers, R. (1996) 'From Ideas to Practice: the Pardido dos Trabalhandos and Participatory Governance', *Latin American Perspectives 23,* Fall.

American Youth Policy Forum (1998) *A Revolution in School District Governance*, Forum Brief, American Youth Policy Forum (www.aqpf. org/forumbriefs/1998/fb121198.htm).

Arnstein, S. (1969) 'A ladder of participation', *Journal of the American Institute of Planners*, vol 35, no 4, pp 216–224.

Association of Community Workers (2001) *Community work skills manual*, Newcastle: Association of Community Workers.

Attwood, M., Pedler, M., Pritchard, S. and Wilkinson, D. (2003) *Leading change: A guide to whole systems working*, Bristol: The Policy Press.

Balloch, S. and Taylor, M. (eds) (2001) *Partnership working: Policy and practice*, Bristol: The Policy Press.

Banks, S. (2003) 'The concept of "community practice"', in S. Banks, H. Butcher, P. Henderson and J. Robertson (eds) *Managing community practice: Principles, policies and programmes,* Bristol: The Policy Press, pp 9–22.

Banks, S. (2003a) 'Conflicts of culture and accountability: Managing ethical dilemmas and problems in community practice', in S. Banks, H. Butcher, P. Henderson and J. Robertson (eds) *Managing community practice: Principles, policies and programmes*, Bristol: The Policy Press, pp 103–20.

Banks, S. (2003b) 'The use of learning journals to encourage ethical reflection during fieldwork practice', in S. Banks and K. Nøhr (eds) *Teaching practical ethics for the social professions*, Copenhagen: FESET, pp 53–68.

Banks, S. (2004) *Ethics, accountability and the social professions*, Basingstoke: Palgrave Macmillan.

Banks, S. (2005) 'The ethical practitioner in formation: Issues of courage, competence and commitment', *Social Work Education*, vol 24, no 7, pp 737–53.

Banks, S. and Noonan, F. (1990) 'The poll tax and community work', *Association of Community Workers' Talking Point*, nos 117 and 118.

Banks, S. and Orton, A. (2007) '"The grit in the oyster": Community development workers in a modernising local authority', *Community Development Journal*, vol 42, no 1, pp 97–113.

Banks, S. and Vickers, T. (2006) 'Empowering communities through active learning: Challenges and contradictions', *Journal of Community Work and Development*, vol 8, pp 84–104.

Banks, S., Butcher, H., Henderson, P. and Robertson, J. (eds) (2003) *Managing community practice: Principles, policies and programmes*, Bristol: The Policy Press.

Barber, B. (1984) *Strong democracy*, Berkeley: University of California Press.

Barnett, R. (1997) *Higher education: A critical business*, Buckingham: Open University Press.

Beard, C. and Wilson, K. (2002) *The power of experiential learning*, London: Kogan Page.

Bennett, N., Wise, C., Woods, P. and Harvey, J.A. (2003) *Distributed leadership*, Nottingham: National College of School Leadership.

Bentley, T. (2005) *Everyday democracy: Why we get the politicians we deserve*, London: Demos.

Bishop, S., O'Brien, P. and Robertson, J. (eds) (2000) *The third sector. Report of event 'Celebrating and developing a coherent strategy for the Third Sector in NE England'*, TUC and One North East, London: TUC.

Blakey, H. (2005) *Participation … Why bother?* Bradford: International Centre for Participation Studies, University of Bradford.

Bolden, R. (2004) *What is leadership?*, Leadership South West Research Report No 1, Exeter: University of Exeter.

Bolton, G. (2005) *Reflective practice: Writing and professional development*, London: Routledge.

Boud, D., Keogh, R. and Walker, D. (1985) *Reflection: Turning experience into learning*, London: Kogan Page.

Boulding, K.E. (1989) *Three faces of power*, California: Sage.

Bourdieu, P. (1992) *Invitation to reflexive sociology*, Cambridge: Polity Press.

Brechin, A. (2000) 'Introducing critical practice', in A. Brechin, H. Brown and M. Eby (eds) *Critical practice in health and social care*, London: Open University Press/Sage, pp 25–47.

Brechin, A., Brown, H. and Eby, M. (eds) (2000) *Critical practice in health and social care*, London: Open University Press/Sage.

Brookfield, S. (1987) *Developing critical thinkers*, Buckingham: Open University Press.

Brookfield, S. (2005) *The power of critical theory*, San Francisco: Jossey-Bass.

Brown, A. and Bourne, I. (1996) *The social work supervisor*, Milton Keynes: Open University Press.

Burns, D., Williams, C. and Windebank, J. (2004) *Community self-help*, Basingstoke: Palgrave Macmillan.

Burr, V. (2003) *Social constructionism*, London: Routledge.

Butcher, H. and Robertson, J. (2003) 'Individual and organisational development for community practice: an experiential learning approach', in S. Banks, H. Butcher, P. Henderson and J. Robertson (eds) *Managing community practice: Principles, policies and programmes*, Bristol: The Policy Press.

Butcher, H., Glen, A., Henderson, P. and Smith, J. (eds) (1993) *Community and public policy*, London: Pluto Press.

Carly, M. and Kirk, K. (2005) 'Citizen participation in local governance – lessons from a network of eight European cities', *Community Development Journal*, issue 7.

Carnegie UK Trust (2006) 'Carnegie appoints Mulgan to chair new civil society inquiry', Press release (March).

Chaffee, J. (1998) *The thinker's way*, Boston: Little, Brown and Company.

Chanan, G. (2003) *Searching for solid foundations: Community involvement and urban policy*, London: ODPM.

Chanan, G. (2004) *Measures of community*, London: Community Development Foundation, Joseph Rowntree Charitable Trust and Joseph Rowntree Reform Trust.

Chinweizu, C. (2006) 'Asylum and immigration: Maximising Britain's economy', *Fight Racism! Fight Imperialism!*, no 190 (April/May).

Clark, M.E. (1990) *Rethinking the curriculum*, Westport: Greenwood Publishing Group.

Cohen, C. and Fung, A. (2004) 'The radical democratic project', in *Swiss Political Science Review*, vol 10, no 4 (Winter), pp 147–210.

Cohen, S., Humphries, B. and Mynott, E. (eds) (2002) *From immigration controls to welfare controls*, London: Routledge.

Commission on Social Justice (1994) *Social justice: Strategies for national renewal*, London: Commission on Social Justice/Institute for Public Policy Research.

Community Development Foundation (2005) 'The Countryside Agency's Community Development Worker programme,' CDF mimeo.

Community Development Foundation (with Community Development Exchange, Federation for Community Development Learning and the Community Development Challenge working group) (2006) *The community development challenge*, London: CDF Publications.

Connelly, S. (2006) 'Looking inside public involvement: how is it made so ineffective and can we change this?' *Community Development Journal*, vol 41, no 1, pp 13–24.

Cooperatives UK (2006a) Somali Development Services (www.cooperatives-uk.coop/live/cme888.htm).

Cooperatives UK (2006b) Minster Housing Association (www. cooperatives-uk.coop/live/cme900.htm).

Darder, A., Baltodano, M. and Torres, R.D. (eds) (2003) *The critical pedagogy reader*, London, RoutledgeFalmer.

Deakin, N. (2001) *In search of civil society*, Basingstoke: Palgrave.

Department for Communities and Local Government (2006) *Strong and prosperous communities*, London: DCLG.

Department of Health (2003) *Delivering race equality: A framework for Action*, London: The Stationery Office.

Department of Health (2004) *Choosing health: making healthy choices easier*, London: The Stationery Office.

Dewey, J. (1986 [1910]) *How we think,* Lexington, Mass: D.C. Heath.

Diamond, J. (2006) *A new view: Distributed leadership*, Usable Knowledge website, Harvard Graduate School of Education (www.uknow.gse. harvard.edu/leadership/leadership002a.html).

Dixon, N. (1994) *The organisational learning cycle*, London: McGraw-Hill.

Dryden, W. and Feltham, C. (eds) (1992) *Psychotherapy and its discontents*, Bristol: Open University Press.

Dweck, C.S. (1999) *Self theories: their role in motivation, personality and development,* PA: Psychology Press.

Elliot, F.R. (1996) *Gender, family and society*, Basingstoke: Palgrave Macmillan.

Fish, D. and Coles, C. (1998) *Developing professional judgement in health care*, Oxford: Butterworth Heinemann.

Fook, J. (2002) *Social work: Critical theory and practice*, London: Sage.

Foucault, M. (2001 [1970]) *The order of things: An archaeology of the human sciences*, London: Routledge.

Frank, A. (2004) 'Asking the right questions about pain: Narrative and phronesis', *Literature and Medicine*, vol 23, no 2, pp 209–25.

Frazer, E. (1999) *The problems of communitarian politics*, Oxford: Oxford University Press.

Freire, P. (1972) *The pedagogy of the oppressed*, London: Penguin.

Freire, P. (1993) *Education for critical consciousness*, New York: Continuum.

Fung, A. (2004) *Empowered participation: Reinventing urban democracy*, Princeton: Princeton University Press.

Fung, A. and Wright, E.O. (2003) *Deepening democracy*, London: Verso.

Gastil, J. and Levine, P. (2005) *The deliberative democracy handbook*, San Francisco: John Wiley and Sons.

Giddens, A. (1998) *The third way: The renewal of social democracy*, Cambridge: Polity Press.

Gilchrist, A. (2003) 'Linking partnerships and networks', in S. Banks, H. Butcher, P. Henderson and J. Robertson (eds) *Managing community practice: Principles, policies and programmes*, Bristol: The Policy Press, pp 35–54.

Gilchrist, A. (2004) *The well-connected community*, Bristol: The Policy Press.

Glen, A., Henderson, P., Humm, J., Meszaros, H. and Gaffney, M. (2004) *Survey of community development workers in the UK*, London: CDF Publications/Community Development Exchange.

Goleman, D. (1995) *Emotional intelligence*, New York: Bantam Books.

Gramsci, A. (1971) *Selections from the prison notebooks*, Q. Hoare and G.N. Smith (eds), London: Lawrence and Wishart.

Griffiths, D., Sigona, N. and Zetter, R. (2005) *Refugee community organisations and dispersal: Networks, resources and social capital*, Bristol: The Policy Press.

Grigg-Spall, I. (1992) *Critical lawyers handbook*, London, Pluto Press.

Habermas, J. (1975) *Legitimation crisis*, Boston: Beacon Press.

Habermas, J. (1990) *Moral consciousness and communicative action*, C. Lenhardt and S. Nicholsen, Cambridge, MA: MIT Press.

Habermas, J. (1996) *Between facts and norms: contributions to a discourse theory of law and democracy*, Cambridge MA: MIT Press.

Handy, C. (1985) *Understanding organisations* (3rd edn), Harmondsworth: Penguin Books.

Hardcastle, D., Powers, P. with Wencour, S. (2004) *Community practice: Theories and skills for social workers* (2nd edn), New York: Oxford University Press.

Hatton, N. and Smith, D. (1995) 'Reflection in teacher education – towards definition and implementation', *Teaching and Teacher Education*, vol 11, no 1, pp 33–49.

Hautekeur, G. (2005) 'Community development and social capital', MA dissertation (mimeo), Leicester: De Montfort University.

Hawkins, P. and Shohet, R. (2000) *Supervision in the helping professions* (2nd edn), Buckingham: Open University Press.

Hayes, D. (2005) 'Social work with asylum seekers and others subject to immigration control', in R. Adams, L. Dominelli and M. Payne (eds) *Social work futures: Crossing boundaries, transforming practice*, Basingstoke: Palgrave Macmillan, pp 182–94.

Healy, K. (2000) *Social work practices: Contemporary perspectives on change*, London: Sage.

Henderson, P. (2005) *Including the excluded*, Bristol: The Policy Press.

Henderson, P. and Salmon, H. (1998) *Signposts to local democracy. Local governance, communitarianism and community development*, London: CDF Publications.

Henderson, P. and Thomas, D. (2002) *Skills in neighbourhood work* (3rd edn), London: Routledge.

Hirst, P. and Khilnani, S. (1996) *Reinventing democracy*, Oxford: Blackwell.

HM Treasury (2005) *Exploring the role of the third sector in public service delivery and reform*, London: The Stationery Office.

Hodgson, L. (2004) 'Manufactured civil society: Counting the cost', *Critical Social Policy*, vol 24, no 2, pp 139–64.

Hofstede, G. (1991) *Cultures and organisations*, London: McGraw-Hill.

Hofstede, G. (2003) *Culture's consequence: Comparing values, behaviours, institutions and organizations across nations* (2nd edn), London: Sage.

Hoggett, P., Beedell, P., Jimenez, L., Mayo, M. and Miller, C. (2006) 'Identity, life history and commitment to welfare', *Journal of Social Policy*, vol 35, no 4, pp 689–704.

Home Office (2004) *Building civil renewal: government support for community capacity building and proposals for change*, London: Home Office.

Home Office (2006) *Asylum statistics: 2nd quarter 2006 United Kingdom*, London: Home Office.

Hope, A. and Timmel, S. (1999) *Training for transformation: A handbook for community workers (Book 4)*, London: ITDG publishing.

Hope, A., Timmel, S. and Hodzi, C. (1994) *Training for transformation: A handbook for community workers*, Gweru, Zimbabwe: Mambo Press.

Hudson, M. (2003) *Managing at the edge*, London, Directory of Social Change.

Humphreys, B. (2004) 'An unacceptable role for social work: implementing immigration policy', *British Journal of Social Work*, no 34, pp 93–107.

Jensen, J. and Miszlivetz, F. (2003) 'The languages of civil society and beyond', CISONET report (draft), Szombathely: Institute for Social and European Studies.

Johansson, H. and Hvinden, B. (2005) 'Welfare governance and the remaking of citizenship', in J. Newman (ed) *Remaking governance: peoples, politics and the public sphere*, Bristol: The Policy Press, pp 101–18.

Johnson, G. and Scholes, K. (1993) *Exploring corporate strategies* (3rd edn), Hemel Hempstead: Prentice Hall International.

Kirkwood, G. and Kirkwood, C. (1989) *Living adult education: Freire in Scotland*, Milton Keynes: Open University Press.

Kolb, D. (1984) *Experiential learning: Experience as the source of learning and development*, Englewood Cliffs, NJ: Prentice Hall.

Lash, S. (1994) 'Reflexivity and its doubles: Structure, aesthetics, community', in U. Beck, A. Giddens and S. Lash (eds) *Reflexive modernization: politics, tradition and aesthetics in the modern social order*, Cambridge: Polity Press, pp 110–73.

Lawton, B. and Felton, C. (2000) *Taking supervision forward. Enquiries and trends in counselling and psychotherapy*, London: Sage.

Learner, J. and Schugurensky, D. (2005) *Learning citizenship and democracy through participatory budgeting: The case of Rosario, Argentina*, Paper presented at the conference 'Democratic Practices as Learning Opportunities', Teacher's College, Columbia University, 4–5 November.

Ledwith, M. (2005) *Community development: A critical approach*, Bristol: The Policy Press.

Leonard, P. (1997) *Postmodern welfare: Reconstructing an emancipatory project*, London: Sage.

Lindblom, C.E. (1968) *The policy making process*, Englewood Cliffs, NJ: Prentice Hall.

London Borough of Harrow (2006) (www.harrow.gov.uk/ccm/content/filestorage-downloads/council-and-democracy/democracy-elections/budgetary-process/hob-final-evaluation.en).

London Borough of Lambeth (2006) (www.lambeth.gov.uk/services/CouncilDemocracy/YouthCouncil/).

Lukes, S. (2003) *Power: A radical view* (2nd edn), Basingstoke: Palgrave Macmillan.

Lupton, R. (2003) *Poverty street: The dynamics of neighbourhood decline and renewal*, Bristol: The Policy Press.

Macmillan, R. and Townsend, A. (2006) '"A new institutional fix"? The "community turn" and the changing role of the voluntary sector', in C. Milligan and D. Conradson (eds) *Landscapes of voluntarism*, Bristol: The Policy Press.

Maslow, A.H. (1968) *Towards a psychology of being*, Hoboken, NJ: John Wiley & Sons.

Mayo, M. (2005) *Global citizens: Social movements and the challenge of globalisation*, Toronto: CSPI, and London: Zed Books.

Mayo, M. and Robertson, J. (2003) 'The historical and policy context: Setting the scene for current debates', in S. Banks, H. Butcher, P. Henderson and J. Robertson (eds) *Managing community practice: Principles, policies and programmes*, Bristol: The Policy Press.

Mercer, N. (2000) *Words and minds: How we use language to think together*, London: Routledge.

Mills, C.W. (2000) *The sociological imagination*, Oxford: Oxford University Press.

Mintzberg, H. (1994) *The rise and fall of strategic planning*, New York: Prentice Hall.

Mintzberg, H. (1989) *Mintzberg on management: Inside our strange world of organisations*, New York, NY: The Free Press.

Moon, J. (1999) *Learning journals: A handbook for academics, students and professional development*, London: Kogan Page.

Moore, D.R. and Merritt, G. (2002) *Chicago's Local School Councils: What the research says*, Chicago: Design for Change.

Nevis, E.C., DiBell, A.J. and Gould, J.M. (1995) 'Understanding organisations as learning systems', *Sloan Management Review* (Winter), pp 73–85.

Newman, J. (2005) 'Participative governance and the remaking of the public sphere', in J. Newman (ed) *Remaking governance: Peoples, politics and the public sphere*, Bristol: The Policy Press, pp 119–38.

OECD (2001) *The well-being of nations: The role of human and social capital*, Paris: OECD Centre for Educational Research and Innovation.

Oliver, M. (1996) *Understanding disability from theory to practice*, Basingstoke: Macmillan.

Olsen, M.E. (1970) *The process of social organisation*, London: Holt, Reinhart and Winston.

Palmer, G., Carr, J. and Kenway, P. (2005) *Monitoring poverty and social exclusion*, York: Joseph Rowntree Foundation.

Pantazis, C., Gordon, D. and Levitas, R. (eds) (2006) *Poverty and social exclusion in Britain: The millennium survey*, Bristol: The Policy Press.

Payne, G. (ed) (2006) *Social Divisions* (2nd edn), Basingstoke: Palgrave Macmillan.

Phillipson, J. (2002) 'Supervision and being supervised', in R. Adams, L. Dominelli and M. Payne (eds) *Critical practice in social work*, Basingstoke: Palgrave, pp 244–51.

Popple, K. (1995) *Analysing community work: Its theory and practice*, Buckingham: Open University Press.

Power Inquiry (2006) *Power to the people*, York: Joseph Rowntree Charitable Trust and Joseph Rowntree Reform Trust.

Pratt, J., Gordon, P. and Pampling, D. (2005) *Working whole systems*, Oxford: Radcliffe Publishing.

Proctor, B. (2000) *Group supervision. A guide to creative practice*, London: Sage.

Putnam, R. (2000) *Bowling alone: The collapse and revival of American community*, New York: Simon and Schuster.

Quinn, F.M. (1998) 'Reflection and reflective practice', in F.M. Quinn (ed) *Continuing professional development in nursing*, Cheltenham: Stanley Thornes.

Ranson, S. and Stewart, J. (1994) *Management for the public domain*, Basingstoke:

Rao, N. (2000) *Reviving local democracy: New Labour, new politics*, Bristol: The Policy Press.

Reid, I. (1998) *Class in Britain*, Cambridge: Polity Press.

Rogers, B. (2004) *Lonely citizens: Report of the working party on active citizenship*, London: Institute for Public Policy Research.

Ronnby, A. (1995) *Mobilising local communities*, Aldershot: Avebury.

Sadler, P. (1995) *Managing change*, London: Kogan Page.

Salford City Council (2006) (www.salford.gov.uk/).

Salomon, G. (ed) (1993) 'Introduction', in *Distributed cognitions: Psychological and educational considerations*, Cambridge: Cambridge University Press.

Salovey, P. and Mayer, J.D. (1990) 'Emotional Intelligence', *Imagination, Cognition, and Personality*, vol 9, pp 185–211.

Sarkar, R. and West, A. (2003) *The LSP guide*, London: CDF Publications.

Schön, D. (1987) *Educating the reflective practitioner: Towards a new design for teaching and learning*, San Francisco, CA: Jossey-Bass.

Schön, D. (1991 [1983]) *The reflective practitioner: How professionals think in action*, Aldershot: Avebury/Ashgate.

Schugurensky, D. (2004) *Participatory budget: A tool for democratizing democracy*, Talk given at a meeting 'Some Assembly Required: Participatory Budgeting in Canada and Abroad', Toronto Metro Hall, 29 April 2004 (http:\\fcis.oise.utoronto.ca/~daniel_schugurensky).

Senge, P. (1990) *The fifth discipline*, New York, NY: Doubleday.

Skidmore, P. and Craig, J. (2005) *Start with people*, London: Demos.

Smalle, Y. and Henderson, P. (2003) 'The manager's role in community auditing' in S. Banks et al (eds) *Managing community practice: Principles, policies and programmes*, Bristol: The Policy Press..

Smith, G. (2005) *Beyond the ballot*, Power Inquiry, York: Joseph Rowntree Foundation.

Smith, M. (1994) *Local education: Community, conversation, praxis*, Buckingham: Open University Press.

Social Exclusion Unit (1998) *Bringing Britain together: A national strategy for neighbourhood renewal*, London: Social Exclusion Unit.

Social Exclusion Unit (2001) *A new commitment to neighbourhood renewal: National strategy action plan*, London: Cabinet Office.

Spender, D. (1990) *Man made language*, London: Rivers Oram Press.

Spillane, J.P. (2006) *Distributed leadership*, San Francisco: Jossey-Bass.

SQW (2006) Briefing Note 1: Participatory Budgeting London (www.sqw.co.uk/pdfs/NM_Briefing_Note-Participatory_Budgeting_F_2.pdf).

Stark, R. (1996) *Sociology* (6th edn), Belmont, CA: Wadsworth Publishing Co.

Taylor, C. (1985) *Philosophy and the human sciences; Philosophical Papers 2*, Cambridge: Cambridge University Press.

Taylor, C. and White, S. (2000) *Practising reflexivity in health and welfare*, Buckingham: Open University Press.

Taylor, M. (2003) *Public policy in the community*, Basingstoke: Palgrave Macmillan.

Taylor, M. and Wilson, M. (2006) *The importance of the neighbourhood*, York: Joseph Rowntree Foundation.

Thompson, N. (2003) *Promoting equality: Challenging discrimination and oppression*, Basingstoke: Palgrave Macmillan.

Thompson, N. (2001) *Anti-discriminatory practice*, Basingstoke: Palgrave Macmillan.

Thornton, P. and Tozer, R. (1994) *Involving older people in evaluating community care: A review of the evidence*, York: Social Policy Research Unit.

Townsend, P. and Davidson, N. (1988) *Inequalities in health: The Black Report*, London: Penguin.

Trompenaars, F. (1997) *Riding the waves of culture: Understanding cultural diversity in business*, London: Nicholas Brealey Publishing Ltd.

United Nations (2004) *72 frequently asked questions about participatory budgeting*. Urban governance toolkit series. Global Campaign on Urban Governance, UN-Habitat, Kenya.

Vaill, P.B. (1996) *Learning as a way of being*, San Francisco, CA: Jossey-Bass.

Walker, A. and Walker, C. (eds) (1997) *Britain divided: The growth of social exclusion in the 1980s and 1990s*, London: Child Poverty Action Group.

Weber, M. (1947) *The theory of social and economic organization*, New York: Oxford University Press.

Wenger, E. (1998) *Communities of practice: Learning, meaning and identity*, Cambridge: Cambridge University Press.

Wilkinson, D. and Appelbee, E. (1999) *Implementing holistic government: Joined-up action on the ground*, Bristol: The Policy Press.

Wilkinson, R. (1996) *Unhealthy societies*, London: Routledge.

Williams, C. (2005) 'A critical evaluation of hierarchical representations of community involvement: Some lessons from the UK', *Community Development Journal*, vol 40, no 1, pp 30–8.

Williams, C., Burns, D. and Windebank, J. (2004) *Community self-help*, Basingstoke: Palgrave Macmillan.

Wilson, M. and Wilde, P. (2001) *Building practitioner strengths: Reflecting on community development practice*, London: Community Development Foundation.

World Bank (2001) *Case Study 2: Porto Alegre, Brazil, participatory approaches to budgeting and public expenditure management*, Participation Thematic Group, Social Development Department, Washington, DC.

World Bank (2006) *Tools and practices 6: Participatory budgeting* (www.worldbank.org/prem/poverty/empowerment/toosprac/tool06.pdf).

Yarnit, M. (2005) 'Blackburn: a Testbed Learning Community' (www.renewal.net).

Zetter, R., Griffiths, D. and Sigona, N. (2005) 'Social capital or social exclusion? The impact of asylum-seeker dispersal on UK refugee community organisations', *Community Development Journal*, vol 40, no 2, pp 169–81.

Index

CRITICAL COMMUNI
PRACTICE

Hugh Butcher, Sarah Banks, Paul Henderson
with Jim Robertson

First published in Great Britain in 2007 by

The Policy Press
University of Bristol
Fourth Floor
Beacon House
Queen's Road
Bristol BS8 1QU
UK

Tel +44 (0)117 331 4054
Fax +44 (0)117 331 4093
e-mail tpp-info@bristol.ac.uk
www.policypress.org.uk

© Hugh Butcher, Sarah Banks, Paul Henderson, Jim Robertson 2007

British Library Cataloguing in Publication Data
A catalogue record for this book is available from the British Library.

Library of Congress Cataloging-in-Publication Data
A catalog record for this book has been requested.

ISBN 978 1 86134 791 6 (paperback)
ISBN 978 1 86134 792 3 (hardback)

Hugh Butcher is an independent consultant in community practice and higher education development. **Sarah Banks** is Professor in the School of Applied Social Sciences, University of Durham. **Paul Henderson** is a community development consultant. **Jim Robertson** was Senior Lecturer in Community and Social Work Studies at Northumbria University.

The right of Hugh Butcher, Sarah Banks, Paul Henderson and Jim Robertson to be identified as the authors of this work has been asserted by them in accordance with the 1988 Copyright, Designs and Patents Act.

Cover design by Qube Design Associates, Bristol.
Printed and bound in Great Britain by Hobbs the Printers, Southampton.